Goal Skeletons

Goal Skeletons

Matthew Petchinsky

1

Goal Skeletons: Build Minimalist Frameworks for Resolutions That Last

By: Matthew Petchinsky

Disclaimer

This book is for educational, informational, and inspirational purposes only.

It is not intended to diagnose, treat, cure, or prevent any medical, psychological, financial, or personal condition. The practices, strategies, and concepts presented in *Goal Skeletons – Build Minimalist Frameworks for Resolutions That Last* are general in nature and may not be appropriate for every individual, situation, or circumstance.

Nothing in this book should be interpreted as medical advice, mental-health counseling, psychological treatment, financial guidance, legal instruction, or professional coaching. **Always consult with licensed professionals**—including physicians, mental-health providers, financial advisors, accountants, or legal experts—before beginning any new health plan, mindset practice, behavior change, habit system, productivity strategy, or lifestyle shift.

The author and publisher disclaim any liability for loss, injury, or damage allegedly arising from the use or application of the information contained in this text. Your choices, interpretations, and outcomes are your responsibility, and results will vary based on personal effort, environment, timing, and individual history.

By reading this book, you acknowledge that you are responsible for your own decisions and that you will seek professional support whenever needed. This book is meant to empower, inspire, and provide clear minimalist frameworks—but **your well-being, safety, and financial stability always come first.**

Introduction

Complexity kills momentum. When a goal becomes too heavy, too crowded, or too tangled with unnecessary steps, it collapses long before transformation can happen. You've seen it: the grand resolutions that shine brightly on January 1st, only to dissolve under the pressure of real life by February. It's not failure—it's overload. Human beings do not thrive inside bloated systems. We thrive inside **simple, breathable frameworks** that make sustainable action possible.

Goal Skeletons was built to solve this exact problem.

Most self-improvement advice wants you to add more—more habits, more routines, more steps, more worksheets, more commitments. But the truth is that success rarely comes from piling more weight onto your life. It comes from **stripping away everything that doesn't matter**, revealing the essential bones of what will actually carry you forward.

Just as a skeleton supports the entire body with elegant simplicity, a **Goal Skeleton** supports your resolution using only the minimum structures required:

- A clear intention
- A simple pathway
- A repeatable habit
- A realistic environment
- A built-in method of staying aligned

Everything else is optional. Everything else is noise.

Minimalist goal design isn't about doing less—it's about **removing friction so you can finally do what matters**. When you eliminate unnecessary steps, decisions, and clutter, you free up immense cognitive bandwidth. You stop arguing with yourself. You stop stalling. You stop feeling overwhelmed before you even begin.

Your goals stop being complicated projects... and start becoming quiet, reliable systems that hold shape all year long.

This book will teach you how to design these systems from the ground up. You won't be given dozens of tasks or massive lists to memorize. Instead, you will build your resolutions like an architect: with strong foundations, minimal materials, clean lines, and predictable durability. You will discover how to identify goal-weight that must be stripped away, how to simplify daily execution, and how to maintain momentum without burnout.

In the pages ahead, you'll learn how to:

- Create resolutions that don't collapse under pressure
- Remove complexity until your goals become effortless
- Build frameworks that support long-term consistency
- Transform motivation into structure—and structure into results
- Keep momentum alive even during difficult seasons
- Maintain alignment using simple, low-maintenance systems

Your life doesn't need more chaos. It needs more clarity.
Your goals don't need more parts. They need more **purpose**.
Your future doesn't need a thousand steps. It needs a **skeleton strong enough to carry you**.

Let this book be your blueprint for resolutions that no longer break, unravel, or fade. By simplifying your goals to their essential frameworks, you'll do more, stress less, and unlock a level of consistency that complexity has stolen from you for far too long.

The year ahead is yours to shape—one simple, powerful skeleton at a time.

Chapter 1: The Anatomy of a Goal – Identifying Vital Bones

The Skeleton Theory: Why Structure Outperforms Inspiration

Most people build their goals backward. They start with a burst of inspiration—a moment of emotional fire—and then try to assemble their plan around that unstable spark. Inspiration feels powerful, but it is chemically short-lived, disappearing long before the real work begins. When a goal is built on excitement instead of structure, it collapses the moment life becomes heavy. The goal was never weak; its foundation was. This is why early motivation must be converted into framework, not relied upon as fuel.

A solid goal begins with a skeleton, a set of essential bones that hold the intention upright even when motivation fades. These bones include clarity, purpose, realistic scale, and minimal complexity. Each element acts as a stabilizing structure. When the skeleton is strong, the goal can stand through emotional fluctuations, seasonal changes, and unexpected disruptions. The problem isn't that people lack discipline—it's that their resolutions lack structure. Strong structure compensates for weak moments.

The skeleton theory teaches that **simplicity is strength**. A skeleton is not cluttered with unnecessary parts; it contains only the pieces required for stability. Your goals should follow the same principle. Strip away the soft tissue of perfectionism, vague intentions, and unrealistic timelines, and what remains is a clean, durable framework you can work with daily. When the internal structure is right, execution becomes lighter and more aligned.

In inspiration-based goal-setting, collapse is inevitable. But in structure-based goal-setting, collapse becomes rare. A well-built skeleton can survive fatigue, low-energy seasons, distractions, and setbacks because it doesn't rely on emotional highs to function. This first shift—moving from emotional fire to structural bones—is the foundation for goals that last all year rather than goals that crumble by February.

The Four Vital Bones: Intention, Scale, Focus, and Purpose

Every resolution requires four vital bones that determine whether it will stand or collapse. The first is **clear intention**, which identifies what you truly want, not what you think you should want. An unclear intention creates instability because the goal keeps shifting. The second bone is **realistic scale**—the goal must fit your current life, not a fantasy version of your life. Oversized goals fracture under real-world stress.

The third vital bone is **focus**, which narrows your attention to the core outcome without unnecessary branches. When a goal tries to grow in five directions, it loses structural integrity. Focus ensures energy flows cleanly. The fourth bone is **purpose**—the emotional anchor that gives the goal meaning. Purpose is not the same as motivation. Purpose is quieter, deeper, and far more durable. It keeps the goal alive even when external excitement fades.

These four bones form the simplest blueprint for a resolution. Without intention, the goal has no direction. Without realistic scale, it becomes too heavy. Without focus, it becomes scattered. Without purpose, it becomes hollow. When one bone is missing, the entire structure becomes unstable. When all four are present, the goal has the strength to endure pressure.

Most people overbuild or underbuild. They load their goal with unnecessary tasks, side-quests, and minor details that drain energy without contributing to the outcome. Or they attempt a massive change without enough structural clarity to support it. Returning to the four vital bones corrects both problems. It restores simplicity, alignment, and stability.

When you build your resolutions around these bones, you stop relying on willpower and start relying on framework. A strong skeleton reduces friction, increases consistency, and ensures your goal is light enough to carry through real life, not just ideal circumstances. These four bones are the difference between a collapsible goal and a sustainable one.

Stress Testing Your Goal: Why Early Collapse Predictors Matter

Before you commit to a resolution, you must stress test it like an architect testing the load-bearing walls of a new structure. The first question is: Will this goal survive pressure? Pressure comes from fatigue, stress, emotional dips, seasonal changes, and the inevitable chaos of life. Goals that depend on perfect conditions collapse instantly when life becomes imperfect. Stress testing exposes weaknesses before they become failures.

One common collapse predictor is **dependency on ideal motivation**. If your resolution requires you to feel inspired daily, it has already failed. Another collapse point is **multi-step overload**—too many tasks, too many moving parts, or too many new habits at once. This creates immediate friction and leads to burnout. Stress testing ensures your goal is light, stable, and resistant to fluctuation.

A proper stress test also examines your environment. If your goal depends on conditions you do not control, the structure is at risk. For example: "I will wake up at 4 a.m. every day" fails if your home environment is loud, unstable, or unpredictable. "I will exercise for two hours daily" fails if your schedule cannot support that load. Stress testing reveals whether the skeleton fits your actual life, not your imagined ideal.

When you eliminate collapse points early, your resolution becomes resilient. It can bend without breaking. It can weaken without shattering. A stress-tested goal gives you stability even when energy dips, moods shift, or life interferes. This is how you create resolutions that don't fall apart—they are built with collapse resistance baked into the foundation.

Turning Motivation Into Structure: The First Transformation Layer

Motivation is not a strategy—it is raw fuel. Dangerous fuel. The early excitement you feel when setting a goal is real, but it is also unreliable. It spikes, fades, and returns unpredictably. If your goal depends on motivation, it will collapse at the first sign of emotional turbulence. The solution is to transform motivation into structure before it evaporates. Structure is what remains after the excitement fades.

The first transformation is converting emotion into clarity. Use your initial motivation to define the "why," the "what," and the "how minimal can this be?" Excitement turns into architecture when you translate it into simple frameworks. The second transformation is converting motivation into predictable pathways. Instead of saying "I'm excited," you create a minimal action that can be repeated regardless of mood.

The third transformation is converting motivation into a **daily or weekly anchor**—a single commitment that stays consistent even when life doesn't. This anchor becomes the heartbeat of your goal. The fourth transformation is converting motivation into environmental design. You use your early excitement to set up systems, tools, reminders, and surroundings that support the behavior long after motivation disappears.

This transformation layer is the difference between short bursts of effort and long-term results. Motivation pushes you to begin, but structure carries you forward. When you turn emotional fire into clean frameworks, the goal develops durability. It becomes a living skeleton capable of surviving your bad days, your busy seasons, and your low-energy periods. Structure is your future self's safety net.

Identifying Collapse Points: What Makes Goals Break Prematurely

Goals break for predictable reasons, and once you know those reasons, you can prevent them in advance. One common collapse point is **uncertain intention**—if you don't know exactly what the goal is, your brain cannot organize around it. Another collapse point is **overestimation of capacity**—people often assume they can do more than they realistically can in their current environment. This disconnect causes the resolution to fracture under pressure.

A third collapse point is **invisible obstacles**—habits, patterns, emotional cycles, or circumstances you didn't account for. For example, trying to wake up earlier without addressing nighttime habits. Or trying to save money without addressing emotional spending triggers. When invisible obstacles go unaddressed, they silently sabotage progress. Collapse becomes unavoidable.

A fourth collapse point is **goal inflation**, where the intention starts small but grows into a complicated monster. "Walk three times a week" becomes "walk every day, then run, then meal prep, then do a full wellness overhaul." Inflation sounds productive but destroys stability. Simplicity always outperforms expansion in the early phase of a resolution.

The final collapse point is **lack of quarterly regeneration**—goals become brittle if they never evolve. Life shifts, seasons shift, energy shifts. A goal that worked in January may not work in April. Without periodic adjustments, even strong goals eventually break. Identifying these collapse points allows you to build a skeleton that bends, adapts, and survives.

The Essential Goal Blueprint: Building a Skeleton That Survives All Year

Your goal blueprint should be simple enough to recall without a notebook, calendar, or app. A durable goal skeleton contains five essential elements: intention, focus, scale, anchor behavior, and alignment check. These are the minimum bones required to keep a resolution alive through the year. If your goal contains more than this framework, strip it down until the structure feels breathable again.

The intention tells you where you're going. The focus tells you what matters most. The scale determines the size and weight of the goal. The anchor behavior ensures progress even when everything else is chaotic. And the alignment check ensures you stay connected to the purpose behind your resolution. Together, these pieces create a lightweight and resilient skeleton.

A blueprint this simple is not fragile. It doesn't require perfect execution, high energy, or intense discipline. It adapts to your life rather than demanding your life adapt to it. The more minimal the blueprint, the more sustainable the goal becomes. This minimalism is not laziness—it is strategic architecture.

When you design your resolutions with an essential blueprint, collapse becomes unlikely. You no longer depend on inspiration. You no longer lose momentum after disruptions. You no longer have to rebuild from scratch every time life knocks you off track. You simply return to the skeleton—the structure that holds everything together.

Twenty Lessons From Chapter 1

1. Motivation is temporary; structure is permanent.
2. Every goal needs a skeleton—intention, scale, focus, and purpose.
3. Complexity weakens the structural integrity of a resolution.
4. A goal must fit your real life, not an ideal fantasy version of your life.
5. Stress testing prevents collapse before it happens.
6. Emotion is not architecture; clarity is.
7. Minimalist goals survive longer because they require less energy.
8. Oversized goals fracture under everyday pressure.
9. Focus channels energy toward progress instead of dispersion.
10. Purpose sustains effort long after motivation fades.
11. Invisible obstacles must be addressed for a goal to stand.
12. Environmental design strengthens a goal's skeleton.
13. Quarterly regeneration prevents brittleness.
14. Anchor behaviors create stability during low-energy seasons.
15. Goal inflation destroys consistency.
16. Early intention determines long-term sustainability.
17. Simplicity is not weakness—it is strategic endurance.
18. Structure transforms effort into cumulative results.
19. A clear skeleton eliminates decision fatigue.
20. Strong goals bend without breaking.

Exercises:

Exercise 1: Identify the Bones of Your Current Goal
Write down one goal you want to achieve. Then answer:

- What is the intention?
- What is the realistic scale?
- What is the main focus?
- What is the purpose behind it?
  Remove any detail that does not support these four bones.

Exercise 2: Stress Test the Resolution
Ask yourself:

- What would make this goal collapse?
- What friction points will appear during busy or emotional seasons?
- Which parts feel too heavy or unrealistic?
  Modify the goal until it feels durable and lightweight.

Exercise 3: Transform Motivation Into Structure
During a moment of inspiration, immediately write:

- One anchor behavior
- One environmental adjustment
- One simplified pathway
  Convert your emotional fire into solid framework before it fades.

Ten Journal Prompts for Chapter 1

1. What goal in my life collapsed because it had no structure?
2. Which part of goal-setting overwhelms me the most?
3. Where does my motivation usually disappear, and why?
4. What does a "lightweight goal" look like for me?
5. What unnecessary details can I strip away from my current resolutions?
6. Which bone—intention, scale, focus, or purpose—has been missing in past goals?
7. What environment changes would support my goals more effectively?
8. How can I simplify my path without losing progress?
9. What fear arises when I think about making my goals smaller and more minimal?
10. What would my year look like if my goals never collapsed?

Closing Reflection — Chapter 1: The Anatomy of a Goal

Clarity is the beginning of every sustainable transformation. In this chapter, you discovered that goals don't collapse because you're weak—they collapse because they're built without structure. When you strip away emotional bursts and create a skeleton rooted in intention, scale, focus, and alignment, you give your resolutions a foundation strong enough to survive the year.

As you move forward, remember that the first build is not the final build. Your initial structure is simply the container that holds your direction. What matters most is that your goal can stand on its own. You don't need perfect motivation or perfect discipline. You need a skeleton that is simple, honest, and capable of holding your future self. The bones you choose now will determine how far you can grow later.

Chapter 2: Stripping the Flesh – Removing Unnecessary Details

The Weight of Too Much: Why Overbuilt Goals Fail

Most goals don't fail because the intention was wrong—they fail because they are buried under too many layers. Every added task, expectation, rule, and timeline becomes another piece of "flesh" suffocating the clean structure underneath. People believe the more complex a plan is, the more impressive or effective it becomes. But complexity does not strengthen commitment; it **strangles** it. A goal bloated with extras becomes too heavy to carry past the first wave of enthusiasm.

The human brain is wired for efficient pathways. When a goal demands dozens of steps, multiple systems, or constant decision-making, the brain responds with resistance. This resistance isn't laziness—it's a protective mechanism against overwhelm. The more complicated your resolution becomes, the more friction appears, and friction kills consistency. Most people mistake friction for personal failure, when the real problem is structural clutter.

A lightweight goal naturally reduces resistance. When the path is simple, your brain doesn't fight it. The action becomes easier to start, easier to maintain, and easier to pick back up after a setback. Stripping away unnecessary details doesn't make the goal weaker; it makes it more **execution-friendly**. You aren't lowering your standards—you're removing the barriers that prevent success.

When you understand that simplicity is a psychological advantage, not a limitation, you begin to reshape the way you design your resolutions. You stop equating "more" with "better." You recognize that your energy is precious, and the goal should serve you—not drain you. This marks the beginning of building an effortless path: not by adding strength, but by removing weight.

The Art of Subtraction: Designing by Removing, Not Adding

Most people begin goal-setting with addition—adding habits, adding routines, adding tasks, adding expectations. But high-performing individuals understand that the real magic lies in subtraction. The art of subtraction means identifying which components are essential and stripping away everything else. It is a creative process of reducing until your goal becomes clean, breathable, and naturally sustainable.

Subtraction requires honesty. You must evaluate which parts of the goal genuinely contribute to progress and which parts simply make the plan look impressive. Many of the things people consider necessities—strict schedules, daily perfection, complex tracking systems—are actually forms of performance, not progress. Removing these elements does not take away from the goal; it liberates it.

When you design through subtraction, you create goals that align with your energy, bandwidth, and lifestyle. This minimizes the psychological resistance that makes most resolutions collapse. Removing unnecessary layers also gives you clarity—you can see what the goal is without the fog of complications. And clarity is the birthplace of consistency.

The art of subtraction is not a one-time purge—it is a continuous practice. Throughout the year, you will revisit the goal and remove new weights as they emerge. As life changes, your systems should shrink, tighten, and simplify to match. Subtraction allows your resolutions to stay alive by ensuring they never grow too heavy to carry.

Clearing the Perfection Fog: Eliminating Unrealistic Standards

Perfectionism is one of the biggest saboteurs of goal execution. It disguises itself as ambition, discipline, or "high standards," but its real function is paralysis. Perfectionism adds unnecessary layers of flesh to your goal: rigid expectations, flawless execution requirements, and punishments for imperfection. These layers create fear, friction, and burnout—conditions that make consistency impossible.

When perfection fog sets in, the goal becomes emotionally heavy. A single missed day spirals into shame. A small deviation makes the entire resolution feel ruined. Perfection makes the goal brittle, not strong. A goal that requires flawless execution will collapse the moment life becomes messy. And life is always messy. Sustainable goals must be flexible, not fragile.

Removing perfectionism involves replacing rigid standards with **minimum viable actions**. Instead of "I will journal for 30 minutes every morning," the skeleton becomes "I will write one sentence daily." The difference between the two designs determines whether the goal survives emotional low points. Minimum viable actions allow progress to continue—even imperfectly.

Clearing the perfection fog doesn't lower your ambition. It raises your likelihood of achieving it. When you stop demanding everything go right, you finally give yourself room to succeed repeatedly. Perfection is heavy; consistency is light. And lightness is what keeps your resolutions breathing through the year.

Reducing Friction: Making Your Goals Nearly Effortless

Friction is the invisible enemy of progress. It shows up in the smallest forms: a workout that requires too much preparation, a daily habit that requires too many steps, a routine that takes too much time, an environment that isn't supportive. Every ounce of friction multiplies over days and weeks, slowly wearing down your ability to continue. A friction-heavy goal becomes unmanageable long before your intention fades.

Removing friction starts with observing your patterns. What tasks do you avoid? Which steps feel emotionally or physically heavy? Where do you pause, procrastinate, or negotiate with yourself? These points reveal where your goal needs simplification. If the workout feels too long, reduce its length. If journaling feels overwhelming, shrink the entries. If meal prep feels exhausting, streamline ingredients. Friction is not a sign of weakness—it is a sign of clutter.

The key to sustainable goals is to remove as many micro-barriers as possible. Reduce the number of steps required. Reduce the amount of time needed. Reduce the level of preparation involved. Reduce the amount of mental effort required to begin. When you build frictionless pathways, the action becomes almost automatic. The easier the first step is, the more likely you will show up repeatedly.

Effortlessness is not laziness—it is strategic design. When a goal is easy to start, consistency becomes natural rather than forced. By eliminating friction, you create a resolution that moves with you instead of against you. A frictionless goal doesn't drain energy; it fuels progress. That shift is the essence of making your resolutions effortless.

Purging Emotional Clutter: Removing Feelings That Weigh Down the Work

Not all clutter is logistical—some of it is emotional. Fear of failure, fear of success, guilt, shame, comparison, doubt, and procrastination often wrap themselves around your goal like heavy emotional tissue. This internal clutter adds invisible weight to even the simplest resolution. Removing unnecessary details means clearing emotional debris as much as physical or procedural debris.

Emotional clutter often forms from past experiences with failure. Your mind remembers the goals you dropped, the routines you abandoned, and the plans you never finished. These memories create hesitation—they tell you not to try too hard, not to commit fully, or not to believe in your capacity. But emotional clutter is not truth; it is residue. And residue can be cleaned.

The process of purging emotional clutter begins with awareness. When you notice fear, guilt, or resistance, instead of ignoring it, name it. Naming the emotion separates it from the goal. You realize the emotion is a temporary feeling, not a structural flaw. This reduces its power over your behavior. You can then design micro-steps that bypass emotional overwhelm.

Removing emotional clutter doesn't require deep therapy—it requires minimalist emotional architecture. Replace shame with curiosity. Replace avoidance with micro-action. Replace fear with structure. When the emotional weight is reduced, the goal becomes lighter, clearer, and far easier to sustain. Emotional minimalism is just as important as task minimalism.

The Minimalist Pathway: Creating Clean, Streamlined Action

Once you strip away the clutter—logistical, emotional, and perfection-based—what remains is the minimalist pathway. This pathway contains the fewest possible steps required to move forward. It is intentionally clean, intentionally light, and intentionally simple. This is where goals become effortless: not by working harder, but by removing everything that makes the work feel heavy.

A minimalist pathway might be shockingly small. One sentence. Five minutes. One walk. One stretch. One micro-habit. But small actions compound. When repeated consistently, they grow deep roots. Complexity creates inconsistency; minimalism creates momentum. The minimalist pathway is not about shrinking your ambition; it's about shrinking the load that carries it.

Creating a minimalist pathway means identifying the one action with the highest return. If a single action gives you 60% of your progress, that action becomes the central pathway. All other steps become optional. When you stop forcing yourself to do everything and instead choose to do the essential thing repeatedly, the goal becomes sustainable.

This is the essence of the minimalist purge: clearing the flesh until only the bone remains. The goal becomes effortless not because it is small but because it is precise. Precision eliminates overwhelm. Precision eliminates friction. Precision transforms the goal from something you "try" to something you naturally execute. The minimalist pathway is the key to long-term success.

Twenty Lessons From Chapter 2

1. Complexity suffocates consistency.
2. Subtraction is more powerful than addition in goal design.
3. Perfectionism adds unnecessary weight to resolutions.
4. Psychological resistance is often a structural issue, not a personal flaw.
5. The easier the action, the more consistent the behavior.
6. Lightweight goals produce long-term success.
7. Friction is the silent killer of momentum.
8. Minimum viable actions outperform perfect routines.
9. Emotional clutter weakens commitment.
10. Simplicity increases follow-through.
11. Goal inflation destroys sustainability.
12. Every layer removed strengthens the core intention.
13. A clear goal is a breathable goal.
14. Consistency thrives in low-complexity environments.
15. Subtraction reveals what truly matters.
16. Effortlessness is the result of good design.
17. Overwhelm is a symptom of excessive detail.
18. Minimalism is a psychological advantage.
19. Removing friction accelerates progress.
20. A streamlined goal is a survivable goal.

Exercises:

Exercise 1: The Subtraction Audit

Choose one goal and list every task, routine, rule, expectation, and requirement you've attached to it. Cross out anything that is not essential. Reduce the goal until the remaining structure feels light and achievable even on your lowest energy days.

Exercise 2: Friction Finder

Observe your behavior for 24 hours. Notice every moment where you avoided taking action. Identify what created the friction—a step that felt heavy, an environment that wasn't supportive, or an emotional block. Remove or redesign that friction point.

Exercise 3: Minimum Viable Action Blueprint

Write down the *absolute smallest version* of your goal's daily action. This micro-action must take less than five minutes and be impossible to overthink. Commit to this minimum viable version for ten days to build effortless momentum.

Ten Journal Prompts for Chapter 2

1. Which expectations do I place on myself that make my goals feel heavy?
2. What parts of my current resolutions feel unnecessarily complicated?
3. Where does friction show up most often in my routines?
4. What perfection standards do I need to release to move forward?
5. What is one action I could shrink without losing progress?
6. Which emotional patterns add unnecessary weight to my goals?
7. What unnecessary "rules" have I imposed on myself?
8. What would my goal look like if it were effortless?
9. How can I make my environment support my goals with less resistance?
10. What unnecessary layers can I strip away today?

Closing Reflection — Chapter 2: Stripping the Flesh

You have now taken the brave step of subtracting what does not belong. Removing complexity is an act of power—one that protects your time, your energy, and your emotional bandwidth. Every layer you stripped away brought your goal closer to its true essence. What remains is the clean, breathable version of your resolution that can actually survive.

Minimalism is not about doing less for the sake of less. It's about clearing the path so your progress becomes effortless. When you remove weight, you create room for momentum. When you simplify, you increase your chances of consistency. Going forward, remember that your goal should feel light in your hands, not heavy on your shoulders. Subtraction is not a loss—it is liberation.

Chapter 3: Ligaments of Accountability – Connecting Habits to Intention

Why Goals Need Ligaments: The Hidden Connectors of Consistency

Goals collapse when there is too much space between intention and action. Intention is the bone—clear, structured, stable—but habits are what allow that bone to move. Without ligaments connecting these two elements, the resolution becomes rigid and brittle. You may have clarity, desire, and a meaningful purpose, but without consistent connectors, the goal cannot bend, adapt, or function in daily life.

Ligaments represent the systems, cues, and micro-practices that attach your intention to real-world behavior. They are not big habits or intensive routines—they are subtle connective tissues that link the why to the what. These connectors give the goal mobility. Without them, even the strongest intention remains theoretical rather than lived.

Accountability, in this minimalist framework, is not pressure, punishment, or external judgment. It is a structural adhesive that reinforces stability. Accountability is best when it is quiet, light, and self-directed. When done properly, it does not shame you into action—it guides you into alignment. It is the gentle reminder that helps you stay connected when life's noise tries to pull you away.

Understanding ligaments is the key to making your goals flexible instead of fragile. A flexible goal survives interruptions. It adapts to stress. It adjusts to energy changes. When your intention is firmly connected to your habits through lightweight accountability structures, you gain the ability to remain consistent regardless of the season you're in.

Micro-Commitments: The Smallest Habits With the Biggest Impact

Micro-commitments are the ligaments that hold your goal together. These are the smallest possible habits—quick, lightweight actions that take less than two minutes but have an outsized effect on momentum. Micro-commitments work because they bypass resistance. They are too small to trigger fear, avoidance, or negotiation. Your brain cannot argue with "one minute," "one sentence," or "one stretch."

When micro-commitments are repeated daily, they create identity reinforcement. Each tiny action communicates to your brain: "I am someone who shows up." This identity shift becomes a stabilizing force in your goal structure. Micro-commitments may seem insignificant, but they create the rhythm that allows larger actions to grow organically over time.

The strength of micro-commitments lies in their survivability. Even on your worst days—when you feel exhausted, stressed, emotionally depleted, or overwhelmed—you can still complete a tiny habit. This prevents the collapse that often happens from all-or-nothing thinking. Consistency continues. Momentum stays alive. The habit remains unbroken.

Micro-commitments should be carefully chosen. They must be simple, frictionless, and directly connected to the core intention of your goal. They are not the whole behavior—they are the anchor point. These anchor habits ensure that even the smallest action moves you in the right direction, keeping your intention tied to your daily reality.

Environmental Accountability: Shape Your Space, Shape Your Success

Environment is one of the most powerful—but least acknowledged—ligaments connecting intention to habit. Your surroundings constantly influence your behavior. They can either support your goal or sabotage it. Most people blame their discipline when the real issue is misaligned environment. When your environment does not match your intention, inconsistency becomes inevitable.

Environmental accountability means designing spaces that make your habits nearly automatic. If your goal is reading, place your book on your pillow. If your goal is drinking more water, keep a bottle in every room. If your goal is financial stability, remove shopping apps from your phone. These small adjustments reduce friction and strengthen the connection between what you want and what you do.

A powerful environment removes decision fatigue. When the tools, cues, and reminders are already in place, you do not have to negotiate with yourself. The action becomes the natural path of least resistance. The cleaner and more supportive your space is, the stronger the ligament between your intention and your habit becomes.

Environmental accountability must be minimalist to be effective. Too many tools, apps, reminders, or systems backfire—they add clutter. A supportive environment is simple: fewer obstacles, fewer temptations, fewer distractions. Design spaces that make the right action easier and the wrong action harder. Your environment will carry you when motivation won't.

Identity Anchors: Becoming the Person Who Does the Habit

Identity is the strongest form of accountability. When a behavior becomes part of who you believe you are, the need for motivation disappears. Identity anchors attach your intention to your self-concept. Without identity alignment, habits remain mechanical and inconsistent. With identity alignment, habits become natural extensions of how you see yourself.

Identity-based accountability begins with shifting from outcome statements ("I want to lose weight") to identity statements ("I am someone who honors my body daily"). The identity itself becomes the ligament connecting your intention to consistent action. When you act from identity rather than willpower, the behavior feels internally motivated.

Identity anchors develop through repetition, not intensity. Every micro-action reinforces the identity. Each time you show up—even for two minutes—you strengthen the belief: "This is who I am now." Over time, the identity becomes so normal that not doing the habit feels more uncomfortable than doing it. This is the ultimate form of effortless accountability.

Identity-based accountability is minimal and powerful. It requires no rigid systems or external pressure. It simply requires consistent reinforcement. When identity matches intention, the goal no longer feels fragile—it feels inevitable. This is how you create goals that carry themselves forward with far less effort than you ever expected.

Accountability Without Pressure: Lightweight Systems That Work

Most accountability systems are too heavy. They rely on high pressure, guilt, or fear of failure. These systems create resistance and eventually lead to burnout. Lightweight accountability removes pressure and focuses on alignment instead. It gently nudges you toward your intention without punishing you for imperfections.

Lightweight accountability may take the form of small check-ins: a calendar mark, a five-second reflection, a simple daily question like "Did I take one step today?" These micro-checks maintain awareness without overwhelming you. They are not about performance—they are about connection. The purpose is to keep your intention visible and alive.

Another form of lightweight accountability is **habit pairing**, linking a desired action to an existing routine. For example: after brushing your teeth, you read one page. After drinking your morning coffee, you stretch for one minute. Pairing eliminates the need to "fit in" the habit—it simply attaches to something you already do. This strengthens the ligament between routine and new behavior.

Lightweight accountability systems succeed because they do not break when life does. They adapt easily. They survive chaos, stress, travel, seasonal shifts, and emotional fluctuations. When accountability is soft instead of harsh, you remain connected to your goal instead of running from it. This softness is strength, not weakness.

The Alignment Loop: Keeping Intention and Habit Connected All Year

Accountability is not a moment—it's a loop. The alignment loop is an ongoing cycle of intention → behavior → reflection → adjustment. This loop ensures your resolution stays alive, relevant, and connected to your daily choices. Without this loop, even the best-designed goals eventually drift out of alignment.

The alignment loop begins with clarity. You revisit the intention regularly to remind yourself why the goal matters. Then you examine the habits supporting that intention. Are they lightweight enough? Are they effective? Are they still aligned with your life? If not, you adjust without guilt. Adjustment is not failure—it is maintenance.

Reflection is a crucial part of the loop. Weekly reflection keeps your habits honest. Monthly reflection keeps your direction accurate. Quarterly reflection keeps the skeleton alive. Reflection doesn't have to be deep—it can be a few sentences or a single insight. But this small act ensures the ligament between intention and habit stays strong.

The alignment loop keeps your resolution sustainable. It prevents drift, collapse, and disconnection. When the loop is active, you are always gently guided back to your path. You don't rely on motivation or willpower—you rely on structure. This loop ensures that your goal not only survives the year but evolves with you.

Twenty Lessons From Chapter 3

1. Habits must connect to intention to create consistency.
2. Accountability is a structural connector, not a punishment.
3. Micro-commitments are the strongest ligaments for daily execution.
4. Small habits produce large identity shifts.
5. Environmental design determines behavioral ease.
6. A supportive environment reduces friction dramatically.
7. Identity is the most powerful accountability mechanism.
8. Lightweight systems outperform high-pressure systems.
9. Accountability should feel gentle, not stressful.
10. Alignment creates sustainability.
11. The alignment loop prevents drift.
12. Micro-actions maintain momentum through emotional low points.
13. Habit pairing creates effortless consistency.
14. Identity anchors make habits natural.
15. Reflection strengthens your connection to intention.
16. Adjustments are maintenance, not failure.
17. Environments can carry you when motivation won't.
18. Accountability works best when it is minimal.
19. Structure, not pressure, creates long-term results.
20. Consistency is the outcome of strong ligaments.

Exercises:

Exercise 1: The Ligament Builder

Choose one goal. Create three micro-commitments that connect your intention to daily behavior. Make them small enough to perform anywhere, anytime, on any energy level.

Exercise 2: Environment Reset

Choose one habit and redesign your environment to make it easier. Remove obstacles, add cues, and simplify the setup. Test the new environment for one week and observe the difference.

Exercise 3: Identity Anchor Creation

Write an identity statement aligned with your goal ("I am someone who..."). Repeat it once each morning. Match it to one micro-action daily to reinforce the identity.

Ten Journal Prompts for Chapter 3

1. Which habits feel most disconnected from my intentions?
2. What tiny action could I take daily that would move me forward?
3. How does my environment currently support—or sabotage—my goals?
4. What identity am I trying to grow into this year?
5. Which accountability systems feel too heavy for me?
6. What does gentle accountability look like in my life?
7. How can I make my habits easier to begin?
8. What environmental change would remove friction instantly?
9. When during the day do I feel most aligned with my intention?
10. What adjustment do I need to make this week to stay connected?

Closing Reflection — Chapter 3: Ligaments of Accountability

Accountability is not pressure—it is connection. It links your intention to your habits, your identity to your actions, your purpose to your daily life. In this chapter, you learned that successful resolutions aren't held together by motivation; they're held together by ligaments that stretch, adapt, and keep the skeleton intact.

Your accountability system does not need to be loud or intense. It only needs to be consistent and aligned. Whether your ligaments take the form of check-ins, identity reinforcement, or small consequences and rewards, they give shape to your goal's movement. As you leave this chapter, remember that accountability is not about perfection—it's about remaining tethered to your purpose, even when life pulls in other directions.

Chapter 4: Muscle Memory – Repetition as Growth

Why Repetition Outperforms Motivation Every Time

Motivation is a spark; repetition is the engine. No matter how inspired you feel at the start of your resolution, that emotional fire will fade. Your progress depends far less on how excited you are and far more on how often you engage with the behavior. Repetition builds familiarity, and familiarity reduces resistance. When a habit becomes familiar, it stops feeling like effort and starts becoming part of your identity.

Repetition also stabilizes your system. Human behavior thrives on rhythm. When your actions repeat consistently, your brain begins to automate the pattern. Automation is the birthplace of ease. This means that repetition is not just about doing the habit often—it's about training your brain to execute the habit **with less energy each time**. This neurological efficiency is how habits transform from draining to manageable.

Many people misunderstand repetition as monotony, but repetition is actually liberation. The more you repeat a habit, the less negotiation you experience. You don't argue with yourself about whether to do it—you simply do it. This removes friction, emotional clutter, and decision fatigue. Repetition frees you from the chaos of overthinking and replaces it with the clarity of automatic action.

Repetition is the great equalizer. Whether you have high energy or low energy, confidence or doubt, discipline or distraction, repetition allows you to keep moving. It doesn't demand perfection—it demands presence. Showing up again and again, even briefly, rewires the brain and strengthens the goal's skeleton. This is how momentum quietly builds until it becomes unstoppable.

The Neuroscience of Habit Formation: How Muscle Memory Forms

Habits form when repeated behavior creates neural pathways in the brain. These pathways begin as thin trails—fragile connections that require conscious effort. But every time you perform the habit, the trail deepens. Eventually, it becomes the brain's preferred route. This is muscle memory at the neurological level: your brain chooses the easiest path, which becomes the habit you practiced most.

Neurologically, the brain loves efficiency. When it identifies a repeated pattern, it shifts the habit from the prefrontal cortex (effort, decision-making) to the basal ganglia (automatic behavior). This transition is what makes habits feel "natural." You're no longer thinking about it—you're simply doing it. This is why even tiny repetitions matter: every repetition is a vote for automation.

Muscle memory also reduces emotional load. When the habit becomes automatic, your brain stops attaching anxiety, guilt, or self-doubt to the action. This emotional detachment makes the behavior smoother and easier to maintain. Instead of forcing yourself to push past hesitation, you glide through the behavior on a neural groove carved by repetition.

Understanding the neuroscience helps you stop relying on willpower. Willpower is unstable; neural pathways are dependable. You no longer need to "try hard"—you simply need to try often. Small, consistent repetition eventually grows into large, effortless transformation. Muscle memory is not accidental; it is engineered through steady reinforcement.

The Power of Tiny Repetitions: The One-Minute Rule

One of the greatest advantages of repetition is that it does not require intensity. A one-minute habit repeated daily creates deeper neural pathways than a one-hour habit repeated inconsistently. Your brain prioritizes **frequency over duration**. This is why the one-minute rule is one of the most powerful tools in habit formation: commit to a version of the habit that takes one minute or less.

The one-minute rule eliminates the biggest barrier to action: psychological heaviness. When a habit feels big, your brain resists it. When a habit feels tiny, the brain accepts it immediately. This acceptance allows repetition to take root. Once the action begins, you may choose to continue longer—but the repetition itself is the win, not the duration.

This rule removes perfectionism, overwhelm, and procrastination. When you reduce a habit to one minute, you are left with the purest form of repetition. You shift from "I must accomplish everything" to "I must simply begin." Beginning is the most powerful part of any habit because beginning reduces emotional friction and activates momentum.

Tiny repetitions are not a compromise—they are the true foundation of long-term success. They create consistency, reinforce identity, and deepen neural pathways with minimal effort. When practiced daily, these micro-habits create the strongest muscle memory of all because they are impossible to avoid and easy to execute.

Riding the Momentum Wave: How Repetition Sustains Progress During Hard Seasons

Difficult seasons will always arrive—busy schedules, emotional turmoil, health dips, family stress, financial strain, or simply fatigue. Most people assume that hard seasons destroy their progress. But the truth is that repetition can carry you through even the hardest periods if the habit is light enough. Muscle memory becomes your fallback system.

When repetition has been established, you don't need high energy or perfect conditions to continue. You only need the strength to do the smallest version of the habit. This is why tiny habits and repetition create resilience. They survive storms. Even in moments when everything feels unstable, the habit remains a familiar anchor that grounds your identity and stabilizes your emotional landscape.

Momentum has its own intelligence. Once you build it, it creates self-carrying motion. A repeated habit becomes part of your day the same way brushing your teeth or checking your phone is. You don't need motivation—it happens almost automatically. This automatic nature prevents collapse during your lowest points.

The true test of a habit is not how well it works on your good days—it's how well it survives your bad ones. Repetition is the only mechanism strong enough to maintain progress when life becomes chaotic. When you master repetition, you become resilient. When the world shakes, your habits remain standing because you've built them into the very fabric of your identity.

Repetition as Identity Reinforcement: Becoming the Person Who Shows Up

Habits are not just actions—they are statements about who you believe yourself to be. Repetition reinforces identity because every action becomes evidence. Every time you perform the behavior, even for seconds, you cast a vote for your new identity. When enough votes accumulate, the identity becomes unshakeable.

Identity-driven behavior is the most sustainable form of growth. When the habit becomes tied to who you are, it stops being something you have to force. It becomes something you naturally protect. Repetition turns "I'm trying" into "I am." This shift eliminates the internal battle between desire and execution. You become the type of person who simply does the habit.

Repetition also breaks identity contradictions. For example, a person may have the goal of being disciplined but still see themselves as inconsistent. Repetition solves this conflict by building a new self-concept through action. You can't argue with the reality of what you repeatedly do. The brain adjusts its self-image to match your repeated behavior.

Identity reinforced through repetition ensures long-term stability. Even when motivation disappears, identity remains. You don't show up because you feel like it—you show up because it is part of your nature. Repetition doesn't just build habits; it builds the person who can sustain them effortlessly.

The Compounding Effect: When Small Repetitions Lead to Big Results

Repetition compounds like interest. Small behaviors, repeated consistently, expand into massive outcomes over time. This compounding is invisible at first. You may not notice the growth day-to-day, but over months and years, the results become undeniable. This is why repetition is the engine of transformation: it makes big goals achievable through tiny, controllable pieces.

Most people underestimate the power of compounding because they expect immediate results. But compounding requires patience and faith in the process. When you trust repetition, you let go of urgency. You stop demanding perfection and begin embracing gradual, sustainable progress. You understand that long-term change is a result of consistent small actions—not occasional large efforts.

The compounding effect also protects you from discouragement. Even if progress feels slow, repetition guarantees movement. A one-minute action repeated daily becomes 30 minutes a month and six hours a year. And that is just the smallest version. Over time, small actions naturally grow. This growth is organic because momentum invites expansion.

Compounding turns your muscle memory into transformation. The habit grows roots, the roots grow branches, and the branches bear fruit. This is how people achieve resolutions they once believed were impossible. Not through force, but through compounding repetition—the quiet strength that builds unstoppable success.

Twenty Lessons From Chapter 4

1. Repetition is more reliable than motivation.
2. Habits deepen through frequency, not intensity.
3. The brain automates repeated behavior to save energy.
4. Tiny repetitions create big identity shifts.
5. The one-minute rule removes psychological resistance.
6. Momentum grows from repetition, not perfection.
7. Muscle memory carries habits through difficult seasons.
8. Repetition stabilizes emotional fluctuations.
9. Automatic habits reduce decision fatigue.
10. Neural pathways strengthen with every repetition.
11. Consistency matters more than duration.
12. Repetition builds resilience.
13. Compounding makes small actions powerful.
14. Identity grows out of what you repeatedly do.
15. The habit survives when it becomes familiar.
16. Repetition removes the need for motivation.
17. Tiny actions are easier to sustain long-term.
18. Habit repetition is a form of self-trust.
19. Hard days become manageable through micro-habits.
20. Success is built through layers of repeated effort.

Exercises:

Exercise 1: The One-Minute Installation

Choose one habit connected to your goal. Reduce it to a one-minute version. Perform this micro-version for seven consecutive days to engrain the first layer of muscle memory.

Exercise 2: Neural Pathway Builder

Pick a behavior you want to automate. Repeat it at the same time each day for at least ten days. Track how the emotional resistance changes over time as familiarity builds.

Exercise 3: Momentum Rescue Drill

Write down a plan for what you will do during low-energy or stressful days. Choose a tiny version of the habit that is guaranteed doable. This becomes your fallback repetition during hard seasons.

Ten Journal Prompts for Chapter 4

1. Which habits have I repeated enough to feel natural?
2. What behavior do I want to automate through repetition?
3. Where do I rely too heavily on motivation instead of muscle memory?
4. What one-minute version of my habit can I commit to daily?
5. When does repetition feel easy, and when does it feel difficult?
6. What emotional barriers disappear when the habit becomes familiar?
7. What identity am I reinforcing through my daily actions?
8. How does my life change when I focus on consistency over intensity?
9. What progress have I made through repetition that I didn't notice at first?
10. What small habit could compound into massive results over the next year?

Closing Reflection — Chapter 4: Muscle Memory

Repetition is the quiet force that carries you through the year. It transforms effort into ease, hesitation into instinct, and habits into identity. In this chapter, you learned that small actions, repeated consistently, carve neural pathways that make your goal feel natural rather than forced.

As you move on, trust the power of repetition. You don't need intensity—you need frequency. You don't need massive effort—you need small daily contact with your goal. Muscle memory is built through gentle persistence, not pressure. When your habits become familiar, they stop asking for negotiation. They simply exist. And when they exist, your transformation becomes inevitable.

Chapter 5: Regenerative Goals – Evolving the Skeleton Every Quarter

Why Goals Become Brittle: The Danger of Static Resolutions

Most resolutions die not because the person failed—but because the goal itself never evolved. A goal created in January is often based on a momentary emotional state, a specific life circumstance, or an idealized version of reality. When life shifts, the goal becomes misaligned. And misaligned goals fracture. Static goals ignore the natural cycles of energy, seasons, mood, capacity, and environment.

Rigid goals become brittle. They cannot bend with your changing responsibilities or emotional landscape. This brittleness causes guilt, frustration, and internal pressure. You begin to feel like the goal is fighting against you rather than supporting you. And when a goal becomes a source of tension, your brain treats it like a threat—something to avoid rather than engage with.

Regeneration solves this problem. When a goal is refreshed every quarter, it becomes a living structure instead of a rigid command. Quarterly evolution allows you to adjust the size, shape, and routines connected to the goal so that it fits your current life. This alignment prevents collapse and restores momentum. A regenerated goal stays light, realistic, and aligned.

Goals are not meant to remain frozen. They are meant to breathe. Like a skeleton that shifts, adapts, and repairs itself, your resolutions must regenerate so they can withstand the pressure of real life. Quarterly regeneration ensures your goals last long enough to transform you—not break you.

The Quarterly Scan: Assessing What Still Works and What No Longer Fits

Every three months, you perform a "goal scan"—a structural assessment of your resolution's vital bones. You examine intention, scale, focus, anchor habits, and environmental support. This scan allows you to detect early signs of misalignment before they become collapse points. What no longer fits must be removed. What still supports you must be strengthened.

During the quarterly scan, you evaluate how your life has shifted. Has your schedule changed? Has your energy decreased? Has your environment become more chaotic? Have new priorities emerged? Even the slightest shift can affect the sustainability of your goal. The scan empowers you to update the structure instead of abandoning it.

The scan also reveals invisible frictions—small stressors that accumulated over the past months. Perhaps a habit takes too long now. Perhaps a routine feels emotionally heavy. Perhaps the original intention no longer resonates. These subtle frictions matter. If left unaddressed, they weaken the goal's skeleton. Regeneration corrects these imbalances.

Quarterly scanning is not about finding flaws—it's about ensuring survival. It is the difference between a brittle resolution that snaps under pressure and a resilient framework that adapts and grows. Evolution is strength. Adaptation is sustainability. Quarterly scans keep your goals alive, functional, and supportive.

Seasonal Alignment: Matching Your Goals to Your Life Cycles

Your life moves in seasons—emotional, energetic, environmental, and situational. Each season demands different capacities. Winter may bring low energy. Spring may inspire creativity. Summer may require more flexibility. Autumn may be a time of reflection. Static goals ignore these cycles. Regenerative goals embrace them.

Seasonal alignment means syncing your goal's intensity with your current bandwidth. During low-energy seasons, the goal shrinks to its simplest form. During high-energy seasons, the goal can expand. This flexibility prevents burnout and maintains momentum. Your goal remains sustainable because it matches your emotional and energetic reality.

Seasonal alignment also honors emotional rhythms. Some seasons feel heavy. Some feel hopeful. Some feel chaotic. Forcing a rigid goal through incompatible emotional periods creates resistance. Aligning the structure with your emotional season creates harmony. The goal becomes something that moves *with* you, not against you.

This alignment teaches you to work smarter, not harder. When your goal adjusts to your life cycles, progress becomes fluid. Momentum remains intact. Growth continues. Regenerative goals honor the truth of your lived experience—and this truth is what makes them sustainable all year.

Lightening the Load: Removing What Became Too Heavy

Every resolution accumulates weight over time. Small habits grow into bigger routines. Extra expectations sneak in. Hidden perfectionism returns. Emotional clutter builds. Even the simplest goal begins to grow "flesh" again. Quarterly regeneration requires removing this weight so the skeleton can remain strong.

Lightening the load involves identifying unnecessary steps that crept back in. Maybe your habit expanded from five minutes to thirty, and now consistency is slipping. Maybe you added side goals that dilute your focus. Maybe you raised the standard too high. These expansions feel productive but quietly suffocate your momentum.

Removing the weight restores the goal's breathability. It brings you back to the minimum viable version—the original lightweight design that made the resolution manageable. Light goals are sustainable goals. Heavy goals collapse. Regenerative trimming prevents collapse by ensuring your goal remains survivable.

This quarterly purge is not retreat—it is maintenance. It preserves your longevity. You are not shrinking your goal because you are weak. You are trimming it because you are committed to keeping it alive. Lightness is not a compromise; it is a strategy.

Reinforcing the Bones: Strengthening What Still Holds

Regeneration is not only about removing weight—it is about reinforcing what works. Some habits have grown stronger. Some routines feel natural. Some anchor behaviors have become part of your identity. These are the bones worth strengthening. Reinforcement amplifies consistency and deepens neural pathways.

Strengthening may involve adding stability tools to habits that feel shaky. It may involve improving your environment to make a habit even easier. It may involve pairing a habit with a new cue to increase automaticity. Reinforcement ensures that the core structure of your goal becomes stronger with every quarter.

This strengthening must still align with minimalism. Reinforcement does not mean expansion. It means sharpening what matters. Refining what works. Removing friction from the behaviors that already feel aligned. Strong habits require less psychological effort—but only if reinforced gently.

When you reinforce rather than complicate, your goal becomes more stable with each cycle. You build a stronger skeleton every season. This is how consistency becomes effortless—not through adding more, but through deepening what already works.

The Regeneration Ritual: Rebuilding Your Resolution Four Times a Year

Regeneration is most effective when practiced as a ritual. Every quarter, you pause. You breathe. You step back and examine your goal's structure. This ritual creates intentionality—it signals to your brain that the goal is alive, evolving, and worth supporting. Rituals anchor identity. Identity anchors consistency.

The regeneration ritual follows four steps: review, remove, reinforce, and realign. Review what happened over the past quarter. Remove what became heavy or irrelevant. Reinforce what stayed strong. Realign the structure with your current life season, energy level, and emotional landscape. These four steps create a living resolution.

This ritual also prevents guilt-based collapse. Instead of seeing adjustments as failures, you begin to see them as the natural maintenance of success. You stop expecting perfection. You start expecting evolution. The goal becomes an adaptive companion, not a rigid demand.

When practiced quarterly, the regeneration ritual makes your goal nearly unbreakable. You don't drop the goal when life changes—you reshape it. The skeleton evolves. It stretches. It adjusts. It continues to carry you forward, season after season, with strength and fluidity.

Twenty Lessons From Chapter 5

1. Goals become brittle when they remain static.
2. Quarterly regeneration prevents collapse.
3. Adaptation is a sign of strength, not weakness.
4. Seasonal alignment makes goals sustainable.
5. Removing weight restores momentum.
6. Regeneration turns goals into living systems.
7. Light goals last longer than heavy goals.
8. Alignment stabilizes consistency.
9. A goal must fit your *current* life, not your past one.
10. Regular reflection prevents drift.
11. Reinforcement strengthens successful habits.
12. Minimalism ensures sustainability.
13. Evolution prevents burnout.
14. Regeneration rituals keep goals alive.
15. Flexibility is a form of resilience.
16. Updating goals is maintenance, not failure.
17. Emotional seasons require structural adjustments.
18. Momentum thrives in adaptable systems.
19. The strongest goals are the ones that bend.
20. Regenerative goals turn short-term intentions into long-term identity.

Exercises:

Exercise 1: Quarterly Skeleton Scan

Review your goal using the five vital bones: intention, focus, scale, anchor behavior, alignment. Identify what fits, what's heavy, and what needs updating.

Exercise 2: Seasonal Shift Mapping

Write down your current emotional, energetic, and environmental season. Adjust your goal's intensity to match your real-life capacity for the next three months.

Exercise 3: Regeneration Ritual Practice

Perform the four-step regeneration ritual:

- Review the last quarter
- Remove unnecessary weight
- Reinforce habits that survived
- Realign the structure
  Do this at the start of every quarter for an entire year.

Ten Journal Prompts for Chapter 5

1. Which parts of my goal feel misaligned with my current life?
2. What became heavier over the past three months?
3. Which habits survived the quarter and deserve reinforcement?
4. What emotional or energetic season am I currently in?
5. What expectations do I need to release?
6. How would my resolution feel if it were redesigned for *today*, not January?
7. What friction appeared recently that I didn't notice until now?
8. What small structural change would make my goal easier immediately?
9. What identity am I stepping into this quarter?
10. How can I design my goal to bend instead of break?

Closing Reflection — Chapter 5: Regenerative Goals

A goal that cannot evolve will eventually break. You now understand that long-term success is not created through rigidity—it is created through regeneration. By reviewing, removing, reinforcing, and realigning your resolution every quarter, you allow it to breathe with your life instead of resisting it.

As you close this chapter, embrace flexibility as a form of strength. Your needs, seasons, energy, and circumstances will change—and your goals must change with them. Regeneration ensures survival. Evolution ensures consistency. Your goal is not a fixed command—it is a living structure designed to support you across every season of growth. Let it evolve, and it will carry you further than you ever imagined.

Appendix A: The 100-Prompt Minimalist Goal Journal

Use these prompts anytime you feel lost, overwhelmed, disconnected from your goal, or ready for a seasonal reset. These reflections remove noise, sharpen intention, and rebuild structure with simplicity and honesty. Each prompt is designed to reconnect you with the "skeleton" of your resolution—its bones, its purpose, and its long-term sustainability.

◈ Section 1: Intention

1. What is the core intention beneath my goal?
2. What do I truly want, without social pressure or expectations?
3. What emotion is driving this resolution?
4. What is the simplest version of this goal that still feels meaningful?
5. What am I really trying to change about my life?
6. What belief is the foundation for this habit?
7. Where did my desire for this goal originate?
8. What does success actually look like for me—not others?
9. What would this goal mean for my identity?
10. What would achieving this goal allow me to stop tolerating?
11. What would achieving it allow me to finally start doing?
12. What personal value does this goal honor?
13. What am I afraid will happen if I fail?
14. What am I afraid will happen if I succeed?
15. What deeper need does this goal fulfill?
16. How can I simplify my intention into one sentence?
17. What part of myself is asking for this change?
18. Who am I hoping to become through this goal?
19. What is the emotional "why" behind this resolution?
20. What intention feels the most honest right now?

◈ Section 2: Removing Complexity

1. What feels unnecessarily heavy about my goal right now?
2. Which steps are actually optional?
3. What part of the process feels bloated or overbuilt?
4. Where am I overthinking?
5. What expectations did I place on myself that I never agreed to?
6. What perfection standards can I release today?
7. What friction makes my goal harder than it needs to be?
8. What tasks can I eliminate without harming progress?
9. What habits feel forced or unnatural?
10. What can I simplify immediately?
11. Which tools, apps, or routines are adding clutter?
12. Where am I adding steps out of guilt?
13. What would this goal look like if I cut it in half?
14. What is the smallest version of the action I can consistently do?
15. What pressure can I let go of right now?
16. What emotional clutter surrounds this goal?
17. What am I trying to make perfect when "done" is enough?
18. What routine would feel more breathable if simplified?
19. What would this goal look like with only 3 steps?
20. What would this goal look like with only 1 step?

◈ Section 3: Accountability & Alignment

1. What small check-in would help keep me aligned?
2. What is the easiest form of accountability for me?
3. Who (or what) can help me stay tethered to my goal?
4. What does alignment feel like in my body?
5. What does misalignment feel like?
6. Where have I drifted from my original intention?
7. What micro-habit reconnects me instantly?
8. What signal tells me I'm going off-track?
9. How can I adjust quickly when I slip?
10. What accountability method has worked for me before?
11. What accountability method has always failed?
12. What habit keeps the skeleton strong?
13. What trigger or cue can anchor this habit in my daily routine?
14. What time of day naturally supports this goal?
15. What environment supports this habit best?
16. What environment sabotages it?
17. What single supportive structure can I add right now?
18. What boundary protects my focus?
19. How will I know when I'm drifting?
20. What alignment question should I ask myself weekly?

◈ Section 4: Repetition, Identity & Momentum

1. What is my one-minute version of this habit?
2. When did a tiny action create big results for me before?
3. What repetition feels natural and sustainable?
4. What repetition feels forced?
5. What habit would be easy to do even on my worst day?
6. What identity am I reinforcing through my daily actions?
7. What identity am I dismantling?
8. What small action makes me feel most like my future self?
9. What habit gives me the most momentum?
10. What breaks my momentum fastest?
11. What three words describe the identity I'm building?
12. What three words describe the identity I'm releasing?
13. How do I behave when I feel like the "real me"?
14. What behavior would the future version of me never skip?
15. What routine makes me feel powerful?
16. What routine makes me feel overwhelmed?
17. How can repetition feel lighter?
18. How can I celebrate tiny consistencies?
19. What tiny win can I achieve today?
20. What habit feels like home?

◈ Section 5: Regeneration & Seasonal Adaptation

1. What changed in my life this season?
2. What does this goal need to look like now—not three months ago?
3. What feels misaligned with my current energy?
4. What feels perfectly aligned right now?
5. What needs to shrink this quarter?
6. What can expand this quarter?
7. What routine needs to be refreshed?
8. What routine needs to be retired?
9. What new rhythm naturally emerged this season?
10. What weight has accumulated around my goal?
11. What can I release today that feels freeing?
12. What habit deserves reinforcement?
13. What is the new "minimum viable version" of my goal?
14. What emotional season am I in?
15. What does success mean *this* quarter?
16. What would make this goal feel easier right now?
17. What do I want this goal to become next season?
18. How have I grown since my last reset?
19. What identity shift do I want to deepen this quarter?
20. What do I want my goal's skeleton to carry for me next?

Message from the Author:

I hope you enjoyed this book, I love astrology and knew there was not a book such as this out on the shelf. I love metaphysical items as well. Please check out my other books:

-Life of Government Benefits

-My life of Hell

-My life with Hydrocephalus

-Red Sky

-World Domination:Woman's rule

-World Domination:Woman's Rule 2: The War

-Life and Banishment of Apophis: book 1

-The Kidney Friendly Diet

-The Ultimate Hemp Cookbook

-Creating a Dispensary(legally)

-Cleanliness throughout life: the importance of showering from childhood to adulthood.

-Strong Roots: The Risks of Overcoddling children

-Hemp Horoscopes: Cosmic Insights and Earthly Healing

- Celestial Hemp Navigating the Zodiac: Through the Green Cosmos

Astrological Hemp: Aligning The Stars with Earth's Ancient Herb

-The Astrological Guide to Hemp: Stars, Signs, and Sacred Leaves

-Green Growth: Innovative Marketing Strategies for your Hemp Products and Dispensary

-Cosmic Cannabis

-Astrological Munchies

-Henry The Hemp

-Zodiacal Roots: The Astrological Soul Of Hemp

- **Green Constellations: Intersection of Hemp and Zodiac**

-Hemp in The Houses: An astrological Adventure Through The Cannabis Galaxy

-Galactic Ganja Guide

Heavenly Hemp
Zodiac Leaves
Doctor Who Astrology
Cannastrology
Stellar Satvias and Cosmic Indicas
Celestial Cannabis: A Zodiac Journey
AstroHerbology: The Sky and The Soil: Volume 1
AstroHerbology:Celestial Cannabis:Volume 2
Cosmic Cannabis Cultivation
The Starry Guide to Herbal Harmony: Volume 1
The Starry Guide to Herbal Harmony: Cannabis Universe: Volume 2
Yugioh Astrology: Astrological Guide to Deck, Duels and more
Nightmare Mansion: Echoes of The Abyss
Nightmare Mansion 2: Legacy of Shadows
Nightmare Mansion 3: Shadows of the Forgotten
Nightmare Mansion 4: Echoes of the Damned
The Life and Banishment of Apophis: Book 2
Nightmare Mansion: Halls of Despair
Healing with Herb: Cannabis and Hydrocephalus
Planetary Pot: Aligning with Astrological Herbs: Volume 1
Fast Track to Freedom: 30 Days to Financial Independence Using AI, Assets, and Agile Hustles
Cosmic Hemp Pathways
How to Become Financially Free in 30 Days: 10,000 Paths to Prosperity
Zodiacal Herbage: Astrological Insights: Volume 1
Nightmare Mansion: Whispers in the Walls
The Daleks Invade Atlantis
Henry the hemp and Hydrocephalus

10X The Kidney Friendly Diet
Cannabis Universe: Adult coloring book

Hemp Astrology: The Healing Power of the Stars

Zodiacal Herbage: Astrological Insights: Cannabis Universe: Volume 2

Planetary Pot: Aligning with Astrological Herbs: Cannabis Universes: Volume 2

Doctor Who: Convergence Protocol – The Replicator War

Nightmare Mansion: Curse of the Blood Moon

The Celestial Stoner: A Guide to the Zodiac

Cosmic Pleasures: Sex Toy Astrology for Every Sign

Hydrocephalus Astrology: Navigating the Stars and Healing Waters

Lapis and the Mischievous Chocolate Bar

Celestial Positions: Sexual Astrology for Every Sign

Apophis's Shadow Work Journal: **:** A Journey of Self-Discovery and Healing

Kinky Cosmos: Sexual Kink Astrology for Every Sign

Digital Cosmos: The Astrological Digimon Compendium

Stellar Seeds: The Cosmic Guide to Growing with Astrology

Apophis's Daily Gratitude Journal

Cat Astrology: Feline Mysteries of the Cosmos

The Cosmic Kama Sutra: An Astrological Guide to Sexual Positions

Unleash Your Potential: A Guided Journal Powered by AI Insights

Whispers of the Enchanted Grove

Cosmic Pleasures: An Astrological Guide to Sexual Kinks

369, 12 Manifestation Journal

Whisper of the nocturne journal(blank journal for writing or drawing)

The Boogey Book

Locked In Reflection: A Chastity Journey Through Locktober

Generating Wealth Quickly:How to Generate $100,000 in 24 Hours

Star Magic: Harness the Power of the Universe

The Flatulence Chronicles: A Fart Journal for Self-Discovery

The Doctor and The Death Moth

Seize the Day: A Personal Seizure Tracking Journal

The Ultimate Boogeyman Safari: A Journey into the Boogie World and Beyond

Whispers of Samhain: 1,000 Spells of Love, Luck, and Lunar Magic: Samhain Spell Book

Apophis's guides:Witch's Spellbook Crafting Guide for Halloween

Frost & Flame: The Enchanted Yule Grimoire of 1000 Winter Spells

The Ultimate Boogey Goo Guide & Spooky Activities for Halloween Fun

Harmony of the Scales: A Libra's Spellcraft for Balance and Beauty

The Enchanted Advent: 36 Days of Christmas Wonders

Nightmare Mansion: The Labyrinth of Screams

Harvest of Enchantment: 1,000 Spells of Gratitude, Love, and Fortune for Thanksgiving

The Boogey Chronicles: A Journal of Nightly Encounters and Shadowy Secrets

The 12 Days of Financial Freedom: A Step-by-Step Christmas Countdown to Transform Your Finances

Sigil of the Eternal Spiral Blank Journal

A Christmas Feast: Timeless Recipes for Every Meal

Holiday Stress-Free Solutions: A Survival Guide to Thriving During the Festive Season

Yu-Gi-Oh! Holiday Gifting Mastery: The Ultimate Guide for Fans and Newcomers Alike

Holiday Harmony: A Hydrocephalus Survival Guide for the Festive Season

Celestial Craft: The Witch's Almanac for 2025 – A Cosmic Guide to Manifestations, Moons, and Mystical Events

Doctor Who: The Toymaker's Winter Wonderland

Tulsa King Unveiled: A Thrilling Guide to Stallone's Mafia Masterpiece

Pendulum Craft: A Complete Guide to Crafting and Using Personalized Divination Tools

Nightmare Mansion: Santa's Eternal Eve

Starlight Noel: A Cosmic Journey through Christmas Mysteries

The Dark Architect: Unlocking the Blueprint of Existence

Surviving the Embrace: The Ultimate Guide to Encounters with The Hugging Molly

The Enchanted Codex: Secrets of the Craft for Witches, Wiccans, and Pagans

Harvest of Gratitude: A Complete Thanksgiving Guide

Yuletide Essentials: A Complete Guide to an Authentic and Magical Christmas

Celestial Smokes: A Cosmic Guide to Cigars and Astrology

Living in Balance: A Comprehensive Survival Guide to Thriving with Diabetes Insipidus

Cosmic Symbiosis: The Venom Zodiac Chronicles

The Cursed Paw of Ambition

Cosmic Symbiosis: The Astrological Venom Journal

Celestial Wonders Unfold: A Stargazer's Guide to the Cosmos (2024-2029)

The Ultimate Black Friday Prepper's Guide: Mastering Shopping Strategies and Savings

Cosmic Sales: The Astrological Guide to Black Friday Shopping

Legends of the Corn Mother and Other Harvest Myths

Whispers of the Harvest: The Corn Mother's Journal

The Evergreen Spellbook

The Doctor Meets the Boogeyman

The White Witch of Rose Hall's SpellBook

The Gingerbread Golem's Shadow: A Study in Sweet Darkness

The Gingerbread Golem Codex: An Academic Exploration of Sweet Myths

The Gingerbread Golem Grimoire: Sweet Magicks and Spells for the Festive Witch

The Curse of the Gingerbread Golem

10-minute Christmas Crafts for kids

Christmas Crisis Solutions: The Ultimate Last-Minute Survival Guide

Gingerbread Golem Recipes: Holiday Treats with a Magical Twist

The Infinite Key: Unlocking Mystical Secrets of the Ages

Enchanted Yule: A Wiccan and Pagan Guide to a Magical and Memorable Season

Dinosaurs of Power: Unlocking Ancient Magick

Astro-Dinos: The Cosmic Guide to Prehistoric Wisdom

Gallifrey's Yule Logs: A Festive Doctor Who Cookbook

The Dino Grimoire: Secrets of Prehistoric Magick

The Gift They Never Knew They Needed

The Gingerbread Golem's Culinary Alchemy: Enchanting Recipes for a Sweetly Dark Feast

A Time Lord Christmas: Holiday Adventures with the Doctor

Krampusproofing Your Home: Defensive Strategies for Yule

Silent Frights: A Collection of Christmas Creepypastas to Chill Your Bones

Santa Raptor's Jolly Carnage: A Dino-Claus Christmas Tale

Prehistoric Palettes: A Dino Wicca Coloring Journey

The Christmas Wishkeeper Chronicles

The Starlight Sleigh: A Holiday Journey

Elf Secrets: The True Magic of the North Pole

Candy Cane Conjurations

Cooking with Kids: Recipes Under 20 Minutes

Doctor Who: The TARDIS Confiscation

The Anxiety First Aid Kit: Quick Tools to Calm Your Mind

Frosty Whispers: A Winter's Tale

The Infinite Key: Unlocking the Secrets to Prosperity, Resilience, and Purpose

The Grasping Void: Why You'll Regret This Purchase

Astrology for Busy Bees: Star Signs Simplified

The Instant Focus Formula: Cut Through the Noise

The Secret Language of Colors: Unlocking the Emotional Codes

Sacred Fossil Chronicles: Blank Journal

The Christmas Cottage Miracle

Feeding Frenzy: Graboid-Inspired Recipes

Manifest in Minutes: The Quick Law of Attraction Guide

The Symbiote Chronicles: Doctor Who's Venomous Journey

Think Tiny, Grow Big: The Minimalist Mindset

The Energy Key: Unlocking Limitless Motivation

New Year, New Magic: Manifesting Your Best Year Yet

Unstoppable You: Mastering Confidence in Minutes

Infinite Energy: The Secret to Never Feeling Drained

Lightning Focus: Mastering the Art of Productivity in a Distracted World

Saturnalia Manifestation Magick: A Guide to Unlocking Abundance During the Solstice

Graboids and Garland: The Ultimate Tremors-Themed Christmas Guide

12 Nights of Holiday Magic

The Power of Pause: 60-Second Mindfulness Practices

The Quick Reset: How to Reclaim Your Life After Burnout

The Shadow Eater: A Tale of Despair and Survival

The Micro-Mastery Method: Transform Your Skills in Just Minutes a Day

Reclaiming Time: How to Live More by Doing Less

Chronovore: The Eternal Nexus

The Mind Reset: Unlocking Your Inner Peace in a Chaotic World
Confidence Code: Building Unshakable Self-Belief
Baby the Vampire Terrier
Baby the Vampire Terrier's Christmas Adventure
Celestial Streams: The Content Creator's Astrology Manual
The Wealth Whisperer: Unlocking Abundance with Everyday Actions
The Energy Equation: Maximize Your Output Without Burning Out
The Happiness Algorithm: Science-Backed Steps to Joyful Living
Stress-Free Success: Achieving Goals Without Anxiety
Mindful Wealth: The New Blueprint for Financial Freedom
The Festive Flavors of New Year: A Culinary Celebration
The Master's Gambit: Keys of Eternal Power
Shadowed Secrets: Groundhog Day Mysteries
Beneath the Burrow: Lessons from the Groundhog
Spring's Whispers: The Groundhog's Prediction
The Limitless Mindset: Unlock Your Untapped Potential
The Focus Funnel: How to Cut Through Chaos and Get Results
Bold Moves: Building Courage to Live on Your Terms
The Daily Shift: Simple Practices for Lasting Transformation
The Quarter-Life Reset: Thriving in Your 20s and 30s
The Art of Shadowplay: Building Your Own Personal Myth
The Eternal Loop: Finding Purpose in Repetition
Burrowing Wisdom: Life Lessons from the Groundhog
Shadow Work: A Groundhog Day Perspective
Love in Bloom: 5-Minute Romantic Gestures
The Shadowspell Codex: Secrets of Forbidden Magick
The Burnout Cure: Finding Balance in a Busy World
The Groundhog Prophecy: Unlocking Seasonal Secrets
Nog Tales: The Spirited History of Eggnog
Six More Weeks: Embracing Seasonal Transitions
The Lumivian Chronicles: Fragments of the Fifth Dimension

Money on Your Mind: A Beginner's Guide to Wealth
The Focus Fix: Breaking Through Distraction
January's Spirit Keepers: Mystical Protectors of the Cold
Creativity Unchained: Unlocking Your Wildest Ideas in 2025
Manifestation Mastery: 365 Days to Rewrite Your Reality
The Groundhog's Mirror: Reflecting on Change
The Weeping Angels' Christmas Curse
Burrowed in Time: A Groundhog Day Journey
Heartbeats: Poems to Share with Your Valentine
Dino Wicca: The Sacred Grimoire of Prehistoric Magick
Courage of the Pride: Finding Your Inner Roar
The Lion's Leap: Bold Moves for Big Results
Healthy Hustle: Achieving Without Overworking
Practical Manifesting: Turning Dreams into Reality in 2025
Jurassic Pharaohs: Unlocking the Magick of Ancient Egypt and Dino Wicca
The Happiness Equation: Small Changes for Big Joy
The Confidence Compass: Finding Your Inner Strength
Whispers in the Hollow: Tales of the Forgotten Beasts
Echoes from the Hollow: The Return of Forgotten Beasts
The Hollow Ascendant: The Rise of the Forgotten Beasts
The Relationship Reset: Building Better Connections
Mastering the Morning: How to Win the Day Before 8 AM
The Shadow's Dance: Groundhog Day Symbolism
Cupid's Kitchen: Quick Valentine's Day Recipes
Valentine's Day on a Budget: Love Without Breaking the Bank
Astrocraft: Aligning the Stars in the World of Minecraft
Forecasting Life: Groundhog Day Reflections

Bleeding Hearts: Twisted Tales of Valentine's Terror

Herbal Smoke Revolution: The Ultimate Guide to Nature's Cigarette Alternative

Winter's Wrath: The Complete Survival Blueprint for Extreme Freezes.

The Groundhog's Shadow: A Tale of Seasons
Burrowed Insights: Wisdom from the Groundhog
Sensual Strings: The Art of Erotic Bondage
Whispered Flames: Unlocking the Power of Fire Play
Forgotten Shadows: A Guide to Cryptids Lost to Time
Six Weeks of Secrets: Groundhog Day's Hidden Messages
Shadows and Cycles: Groundhog Day Reflections
The Art of Love Letters: Crafting the Perfect Message
Romantic Getaways at Home: Turning Your Space into Paradise
Purrfect Brews: A Cat Lover's Guide to Coffee and Companionship
The Groundhog's Wisdom: Timeless Lessons for Modern Life
The Shadow Oracle: Groundhog Day as a Predictor
Emerging from the Burrow: A Journey of Renewal
The Language of Love: Learning Your Partner's Love Style
Authorpreneur: The Ultimate Blueprint for Writing, Publishing, and Thriving as an Author
Weathering the Seasons: Groundhog Day Perspectives
Valentine's Day Magic: A Guide to Romantic Rituals
The Shadow Chronicles: Stories of Groundhog Day
Love and Laughter: Fun Games for Valentine's Day
AstroRealty: Unlocking the Stars for Property Success
The Groundhog's Path: A Guide to Seasonal Balance
Groundhog Day Diaries: Reflections in the Shadow
The Groundhog's Light: Illuminating the Path Ahead
Valentine's Traditions from Around the World
AI Wealth Revolution: Unlocking the Trillionaire Mindset
Love Rekindled: Reigniting Passion in Relationships
Single and Thriving: Self-Love on Valentine's Day
Emerald Legends: Mystical Tales of Ireland
Green Alchemy: Harnessing Nature's Magic
The Hearts of Horror: A Valentine's Day Nightmare

The Leprechaun's Guide to Wealth and Wisdom
Dancing with the Sidhe: Celebrating the Otherworld
Shamrocks and Shadows: Mysteries of the Green Isle
Emerald Energy: Harnessing Luck and Growth
The Gingerbread Golem's Valentine: A Sweetheart's Guide to Love and Enchantment
The Celtic Knot: Weaving Life and Destiny
Green Fire: Elemental Magic for St. Patrick's Day
Clover Chronicles: Finding Your Inner Luck
Ireland's Mystical Creatures: A Field Guide
Gingerbread Golem's Love Almanac
Prowl and Thrive: The Lion's Guide to Success
Love Alchemy: Transforming Your Life Through Heart Energy
WORLD DOMINATION: Woman's Rule 3:The New Life
The Midnight Rose: A Guide to Lunar Love Spells
The Forbidden Letters: Writing Your Own Love Prophecy
Luck and Lore: St. Patrick's Day for Modern Mystics
The Green Path: A Pagan Celebration of Renewal
The Dark Architect's Guide to Reprogramming Reality
Prankster's Paradise: A Guide to Harmless Hijinks
Manifest Your Reality: The Law of Attraction Simplified
The TARDIS Owner's Manual: Understanding the Doctor's Ship: *A complete guide to the TARDIS, its technology, secrets, and mysteries*
Starlit Romance: Astrology Secrets for Finding True Love
The Time Lord's Atlas: A Complete Guide to the Whoniverse: ***A breakdown of the locations, planets, and dimensions explored in Doctor Who***
Sweetheart Shadows: The Dark Side of Love and Attraction
February Fire: Reigniting Passion in Every Area of Life
The Self-Love Toolkit: 5 Ways to Embrace Who You Are
February Sparks: Ignite Your Dreams in 28 Days

March to Success: A 31-Day Action Blueprint
Ancient Paths: The 13 Sacred Principles of Dino Wicca
Echoes of Tomorrow: Navigating the AI Revolution
The Wellness Blueprint: Balancing Mind, Body, and Soul
Green Horizons: Sustainable Living for a Better Tomorrow
The AI Wealth Code: How to Make Millions with Automation
AI-Powered Creativity: Writing, Art, and Music for Profit
Extinction Rites: Rebirthing Your Soul Through Prehistoric Magick
Sacred Serpents tarot
Celestial Enchantment blank journal
Star Strains
Culinary Journeys: Exploring Global Flavors at Home
The Hollowvale Curse
The Hollowvale Harvest
The Egg of Transformation: Awakening Your Inner Power
Blooming Into Power: A Wiccan Guide to Spring Awakening
The Nightmare Nexus: The Third Doctor's Perilous Haunting
Digital Detox: Reclaiming Your Life in a Connected World
Ostara's Path: Walking the Spiral of Renewal
The Sacred Hare
Financial Freedom: Building Wealth in the Modern Age
Spring's Cauldron: Stirring the Waters of Change
The Hollowvale Pact
Quantum Consciousness: The Science of Reality Shifting
The Hollowvale Hunger
The Sacred Waters Within: A Witch's Guide to Hydrocephalus Magick
The Raven's Nest: Building a Life of Unshakable Stability
AI and the Human Mind: The Future of Intelligence
The Hollowvale Reckoning
Timeless Love: Building and Maintaining Lasting Relationships

The Raven's Roar: Unlocking Unstoppable Confidence
Raven Sight: Awakening Intuition and Inner Wisdom
The Butterfly Effect: Small Changes, Big Transformations
Taming the Boogeyman: How to Conquer Your Inner Fears
The Magick of Green: Awakening Earth's Energy in You
The Entrepreneurial Mindset: Secrets to Business Success
The Hollowvale End
The Shadow Luck Ritual: Reclaiming Power from Your Dark Side
Spring Magick for Beginners: A Simple Guide to Seasonal Energy Work
Doctor Who: The Hollowvale Conundrum
The March of Miracles: Unlocking Synchronicities in Spring
Unveiling the Cosmos: A Guide to Stargazing and Space Exploration
The Ultimate Guide to Surviving an Economic Collapse
The AI Gold Rush: How to Profit from the AI Revolution
Bastet's Shadow: The Hidden Power of Feline Magick
The Bastet Codex: Unlocking the Goddess's Magickal Secrets
Purring Spells: Harnessing Bastet's Healing Frequencies
Bastet's Nine Lives: Rebirth, Transformation, and Immortality Spells
Primal Currents: Hydrocephalus Magick in the Path of Dino Wicca
The Digital Gold Rush: Mastering E-Commerce and Online Sales
Future Shock: Adapting to the Next Decade of Change
The Quantum Mindset: Think Like a Billionaire
Sacred Motherhood: Awakening the Divine Feminine Within
The Mother's Spellbook: Enchantments for Love, Protection, and Prosperity
The Witch's Guide to Parenting: Raising Empowered and Intuitive Children

The Magick of Motherhood: Reclaiming Your Power Through Rituals

The Pagan Path to Self-Love: A Goddess's Guide to Worth and Confidence

Wild Woman Magick: Unleashing Your Primal Power

The Money Magnet Blueprint: Unlocking Unlimited Wealth

Biohacking 101: Unlock Your Body's Full Potential

The Wild Father: A Pagan Guide to Strength and Wisdom

The Sacred Masculine: Unlocking Your Inner Power

The Druid's Compass

The Warrior's Mindset

The Father's Fire

Odin's Path

Ancestral Bonds

The House That Whispers

The Magician's Code

The Wild Hunt

The Green Man's Path

The Altar of Success

The Shadow and the Sword

The High Priestess's Guide to Energy Healing

The Lunar Mother

The Sacred Self-Care Grimoire

The Womb Wisdom Codex

The Wheel of the Mother

The Witch's Guide to Manifestation

The Q2 Reset

The Ultimate Guide to AI-Powered Passive Income

Escape the 9-5

AI Feline Fortunes

The Tear-Stained Grimoire

Razorblade Runes

Cemetery Sirens

The Midnight Wristwatch
The Town That Forgets
AI Horror & Creepypasta
The Hollow Frequency
The Breach Echo
The Quiet Between Worlds
The Sigil of Tharan-Khul
Summon the Vault of Y'ha'ten
The Becoming Codex
The Profit of Az'ra-nar
The Drowned Logos
Echoes of the Eldritch Will
The Deep Ledger
Necronomicon of Networth
Covenant of the Wealthwyrm
The Whisperer's Manifesto
The Rites of Azh-K'luth
The Ark of the Crawling Coin
The Tithe of Shadows
Inkheart Abyss
The Timewinds of Y'ha-nthlei
The Spiral Labyrinth of Azag-Nirrh
The Gallifreyan Heresy of the Black Pharaoh
The Psalms of Nyog-Sotha
Black Rain Alchemy
The Infinite Maw
The Entropic Blueprint
The Oracle of Sh'guul
The Book of Breach
The Drowned Saint's Testament
Dreamcraft of the Sleeper God
The Silence Market
Cthonomics: The Dark Wealth Algorithm

Invocation of the Ten-Eyed King
Wealthbound to the Wyrm Below
Become the Unnameable
Codex of the Sovereign Flame
Rituals of Relentless Becoming
The Shadow Ascends
The Eyes Beneath You
The Will That Wakes Worlds
Silence Is a Weapon
The Mirror That Screams
The Whisper Between Moments
The Mind That Devours Fear
The Myth of the Finished Self
The Architect of Your Madness
The Voice You've Buried
The Discipline of Madness
Stormborn: Awakening Your Inner Tempest
The Mind That Ate Time
Unbind Your Becoming
The Pact You Owe Yourself
The Devourer's Diet
The Acid That Carves the Path
The Tower You Must Burn
The Breath Between Worlds
Speak Like the Deep
The Labyrinth Within
The Spine of the Sea God
Rejection Is a Portal
The Crown You Refused
The Scar Is the Spell
The Lightless Flame
The Habit of Becoming Horrific
ChickenJockey Chaos

The Gatekeeper Within
You Are Not Your Name
The Compass of the Mad
The Archive of Unsent Letters
What the Mirror Can't Show You
The Knife You Needed
Worship Nothing, Become Everything
The Other Voice
The Body the World Forgot
The Vein of the Void
The Black Bone Codex
The Puzzle of the Hidden Self (Millennium Puzzle)
The Eye That Sees the Lie *(Millennium Eye)*
The Ring of Return (Millennium Ring)
The Rod of Relentless Will ***(Millennium Rod)***
The Tally of the Soul (Millennium Tauk/Necklace)
The Key to the Locked Timeline (Millennium Key)
The Scale of Sacred Decisions (Millennium Scales)
Inferno Bites: The UnOfficial Minecraft Lava Cookbook
Rot in the Attic
Prana: The Hidden Force of Your Infinite Self
The Shadow Realm Within: Transforming Darkness Into Destiny
The Borderland Collapse
Claws of Protection: Bastet's Defensive Magick
Mr. Ring-a-Ding's Madness
Yugioh Astrology: Celestial Deckcraft and Duel Destiny (2026–2027 Edition)
The Seal You Signed: Unlocking the Power You Once Feared
The Puzzle of Infinite Minds: Unlocking the Mentalism Hidden Within
The Eye That Mirrors the All: Secrets of Inner Reflection
Doctor Who: The Toymaker's Broadcast

The Rod of Eternal Flow: Commanding the Currents of Vibration
Golden Eyes of Bastet: Enhancing Psychic Vision
The Key of Dual Forces: Balance Within the Polarity
The Scales of Living Rhythm: Timing the Dance of Life
The Necklace of Hidden Cause: Weaving the Webs of Fate
The Ring of Secret Masters: Rising Through the All Within All
Daggers of the Dying Deep
Bastet's Wealth and Fortune Magick: Prosperity Rituals of the Goddess
The Tide that Speaks
The Scrolls of Petosiris: 13 Rituals from the Feathered Eye
Petosiris and the Living Plague of Osirion
Feline Fire: Bastet's Passion and Love Magick
The Star Altar of Petosiris
Bastet's Whiskers: Supernatural Sensory Magick
The Bastet Grimoire
Feeding the Shadows
The Mouthless Prayer
The Spiral Wound
Becoming the Ibis: Lessons from Petosiris's Mind
The Crimson Coven: Cola Magick for Sweet Dominion
Sacred Cat's Paw
The Soda Zodiac: A Flavor for Every Sign
Covenant of the Crawling Flame
The Ink of Ish'Zur
Frothroot: The Thirst That Ate the World
The Golden Glyphs of Prosperity
The Etherbind Codex
Echoes of the Resistance: Reclaiming the You That Survived
Harnessed Minds: Breaking Free from Mental Control
The Eyes in the Smoke

Rootwake: The Carbon Covenant
Skitter Logic: Unlearning the Fear That Built You
Doctor Who: The World That Froths
Rootwake: The Fizz That Rewrites Flesh
Rootwake: Frothfather of the World
The Holly Pact: Blood Beneath the Mistletoe
The 2nd Mass Principle: Building Unbreakable Tribes
Web of Wits: A Survival Guide to Encounters with Anasi the Spider (Aunt Nancy)
The Hexbreaking Handbook: Effective Spells to Remove Curses
Pop Alchemy: Transform Your Life One Sip at a Time
The Mason Code: Leading in Unleadable Times
Petosiris and the Fifth Chamber of Thoth
The Ether Seed Within
The Parent of Tomorrow
Petosiris's Pyramid of Perpetual Wealth
Unlearn the World
Grimoire of the Hollow Tongue
Zodiac Weeds: Finding Your Strain Through the Stars
Aquarius Rises in the Bank
The Sugar God's Smile
The Skinclock Reversal: Biohacking the Face of Time
Debtburn: How to Obliterate What You Owe Forever
The Ice Cream Oracle: What Your Cone Says About Your Future
Silence Is Sovereignty: The Power of Being Unreadable
The Wind That Whispers Through Stone
Path of the Four Directions
Doctor Who: The Maestro's Symphony of Endings
Oxygen Grail: Breathing to Undo the Clock
Zodiacal Collapse: When Stars Devour Time
Teachings from the Red Sand Silence

Doctor Who: Omega – The Broken Equation
Memory Wipe Your Past: Start Over Like a MiB
Mitochondria Prime: Ignite the Core of Youth
A Nest of Roaches
Grub from the Galaxy: MiB Recipes You'll Never Forget
Whiskers of Power: Bastet's Guide to Inner Sovereignty
The Gift Must Cost Them: Negotiation Through Unequal Exchange
The Worm Guys' Wealth Code: Hustle Like an Alien
Bug Out: The Edgar Method for Ruthless Goal Setting
Weaving Life with Spiderwoman's Pattern
Doctor Who: The Rani's Renaissance
How to Get a Job (If You're a Puppygirl)
Speak Through Others: The Art of Proxy Power
T-Rex Your Trauma: Reclaim the Power of Your Primal Self
The Black Briefcase: How MiB Stay Wealthy in Silence
The Thirst Beyond Reason: Understanding Diabetes Insipidus From the Inside Out
Backwoods Witchcraft for Billionaires: The Pagan Path from Dirt Roads to Gold Roads
The Moonshine Grimoire: Fermented Spells for Abundance
The Nameless Geometry
The Wraith's Mixtape: Spellcasting with Songs of Sorrow
The Gallifreyan Gentleman: Silent Wealth, Sonic Confidence, and the Doctor's Code of Living
Sugar Water Confidence
Dino Totems: Spirit Guides from Earth's First Gods
Pumpkin Sigils & Ritual Smoke
The Hózhó Compass
The Distortus Discipline – Order from Inner Mutation
Witchcraft for the Cold-Blooded Soul
Moonlight Over the Blessingway
Water, Interrupted: When the Body Forgets How to Hold On

Deformed but Divine: Embracing Your Asymmetry
Hexes in the Henhouse: The Farm Witch's Guide to Power
The Reversed Flame: A Grimoire of Inverted Power
Salt, Cells, and Sanity: Reclaiming Balance with Diabetes Insipidus
King of the Broken: Crowning the Flawed Self
Moonlight Scars: Emo Moon Magick and the Art of Lunar Sorrow
Noose Spells: Magick of the Hanging Rope
The Goth Cathedral: Rituals of the Broken and Beautiful
The Cretaceous Codex: Dino Spirits and Fossil Magick
The Turkey Bones Ritual
Nine Lives of Manifestation: Unlocking Bastet's Reality Codes
Chaos Muscles: Building Strength from Twisted Pain
Emo Blood Magick: The Veins of Power
The 3AM Flood: Nighttime Urination, Sleep Loss, and the DI Spiral
The Silence Between the Stars
The Lemon Method: Sour Your Way to Success
Starlit Sovereign
The Rite of Twelve Gates: Walking the Gates of the Duat.
Cornbread and Conjure: Recipes for Riches and Rootwork
The Black Rose Rituals: Emo Love Spells and Obsession Magick
The Eternal Goodbye: Death Magick and Rebirth Rituals
Sinkrot: The Drain That Remembers
The Hybrid Mindset: Thinking Beyond Evolution
Bone Dry: Navigating Dehydration Before It Breaks You
Wreathcraft: Winter Sigils and Yuletide Spells
The Rite of Twelve Mouths
S'mores of the Damned: Haunted Recipes for Halloween Night

Rethink the Drink: A Beverage Survival Guide for DI Warriors

The Shadow Chord: Guitar Magick and Sonic

Malformed Yet Majestic: Leading When You Feel Wrong Inside

The Cursed Diary: Ink-Stained Spells of the Emo Soul

Anxiety Off Switch: Emergency Reset for a Fried Nervous System

The Energy Heist: How to Take Back Your Life from Drainers

Beyond the Bathroom: Rebuilding Your Social Life With DI

Coyote's Gift for Decision Makers

Ghoul-Goo: Spooky S'mores You'll Die For

Echoes in the Mirror: Scrying and Self-Destruction Magick

Thread and Thorn: Stitching Spells from Rural Cloth

The Mogwai Mind: Building Untouchable Wealth from Small Ideas

Be Your Own Guide: Trust Your Inner Compass

Hormones in Chaos: The Endocrine Puzzle of Diabetes Insipidus

ChronoCleanse: Detox Your Biological Timeline

The Limb You Hide Is the One That Saves You

Leaves, Bones, and Whisper Spells

The Dinosaur Mindset: Prehistoric Tactics for Modern Wealth

Clawing Back Control: A Bastet Method for Boundaries and Empowerment

Samhain Codes of the Forgotten

Orange Alchemy: The Autumnal Spellbook

Monster Within, Master Without

The Sigil That Sleeps

Hearthcraft: Yule Hearth Sigils and Winter Warmth Spells

Temple of the Purring Moon: Rituals from Bastet's Lineage

When the Earth Remembers Your Footsteps

Food for Mood: Eat to Heal Depression, Not Just Survive It
Witch of the Kudzu Vine: Southern Pagan Wealth Secrets
The Invisible Diagnosis: Advocating for Yourself With DI
The Coffin's Lullaby: Sleep Magick and Nightmares as Portals
Ashes of the Will: Rituals for Erasing the Self
The Fracture Rite: Shattering the Magickal Core
Funeral Candles: The Art of Emo Flame Magick
The Black Grimoire: A Blank Ritual for Writing in Absence
Phantom Thirst: A Halloween Survival Guide for Diabetes Insipidus
The Hollow Crown: Emo Royalty and Magick of the Outcast King
Sandpainting for the Soul
Falling Into Balance: Using the Extra Hour to Recalibrate Life
100 Southern Superstitions That Still Work
The DI Child: A Parent's Guide to Raising Hydrated, Happy Kids
The Jungle of Shame: Escaping the Hidden Lab of Doubt
The Witch's Toast: S'mores Spells and Creepy Confections
The Hoodoo Pantry: Spells from the Mason Jar
The Immortal Fortune: Secret Wealth Lessons from Captain Jack Harkness
The Specter's Embrace: Magick for Channeling Ghostly Lovers
Grateful Waters: A Thanksgiving Survival Guide for Diabetes Insipidus
The Seizure Gospel
Harvestbind: Autumn Sigils and Samhain Spells
Doctor Who: The Algorithmic Awakening
Silent Nights, Steady Waters: A Christmas Survival Guide for Diabetes Insipidus
The Extra Hour Effect: How One Hour Can Transform Everything

Blade Between the Breaths

Running with the Mountain Shadows

Echoes of the Failed Experiment – Becoming a Living Legacy

Swamp Witches & River Ghosts: Real Southern Hauntings

Cornbread Prophecies: Magical Recipes from a Southern Table

Doctor Who: The Signal in the Star

Bloomcraft: Spring Sigils and Equinox Enchantments

Vanisher: How to Disappear from the Internet Without Losing Your Life

The Ultimate Christmas Cookie Cookbook

The Unbreakable Parent: How to Mentally Survive Raising Kids in a Broken World

Time Debt: How to Reclaim the Hours You Didn't Know You Lost

One Month, One Million: Unconventional Cash Creation Tactics

Doctor Who: The Cyber Conversion Protocol

Black Friday Frenzy: The Art of Finding Hidden Online Deals

The Grimoire Buried Under the Apple Tree

Digital Couponing Masterclass: Your Step-by-Step Guide to Black Friday Savings

The Fire Inside the Flint

Shadows on the Ceiling: The Emo Guide to Astral Magick

The Bone-Eaters Beneath Us

Black Friday Bundle Blueprint: Creating Irresistible Product Packages for Maximum Sales

Thirteen Nights of Unbinding

Doctor Who: Engines of Influence

Pumpkin Spice Alchemy: Recipes of Fire and Frost

When Raptor Met Rexy: Prehistoric Lessons in Wild Romance

Oblivion's Candle: Burn the Path Behind You

Campfire Curses and Chocolate: A Halloween S'mores Grimoire
The Wallet That Wasn't Mine: Breaking Free from Inherited Scarcity
The Cola Zodiac: What Your Fizz Says About Your Fate
Frostfire Fortune: Unlocking Winter's Hidden Prosperity
Signal Jamming: Detox Your Brain from Info Overload
The Dust of the Forgotten Rite
The Golden Cat Sigils: Drawing Power in Bastet's Name
Mud Magick: The Prosperity of Getting Dirty
Savory Spicefall: Beyond the Pumpkin Pie
Pumpkin Spice Apothecary Kitchen
The Pumpkin Spice Economy: Turning Trends into Billions
The Ember Veil: 13 Nights of Fire Magick
Financial Freeze: When Earning Triggers Panic
The Gingerbread Alchemist: Sweet Recipes with a Twist
Biosynth Power: Programming Yourself from Scratch
Echoes from the Talking Circle
Truffle Alchemy: Fungus of Fortune
Spores of Power: The Truffle Witch's Handbook
Doctor Who: The Tower That Speaks
The Mycelium Veil: Truffle Magick Unbound
Broke But Ashamed: Healing the Shame Wound of Debt
The Evergreen Mind: Growth Through Winter Stillness
The Black Veil Truffle Rite
The Voice Beneath Symbols
Witchlight on the Bayou: Swamp Spells for Sovereignty
I Grew Up Poor and Now I Sabotage My Success
The Lantern of Hollow Souls
Shutdown Survival: A Citizen's Guide to Thriving When Government Stops
When Abundance Feels Like a Threat: Healing the Hidden Fears of Enough

The Scarecrow Grimoire
Owls of the October Veil
Candlewax and Curses: A Halloween Spellbook
Excavating the Inner Fossil – Transforming Fossilized Thoughtforms into Tools of Power
The Yule Witch's Spellbook: Magick for the Holiday Season
Haunted Christmas: Ghost Stories for Winter Nights
The Christmas Survival Guide: Thriving Through the Chaos
The Bone Orchard Rites
Haunted Commerce: The Ghost in the Marketplace
When Money Triggers the Inner Child
Silent Night with the Silence: A Christmas Thriller
The Lightning Crown: Living and Leading Through Seizures
TARDIS Tidings: Festive Stories from the Whoniverse
Autumn Reset: Slowing Down Without Falling Behind
The Trillion Dollar Soul: Rewriting the Currency of Reality
Truffle Eclipse Magick
Micro-Manifestations: Quick Magick That Works
5-Minute Rituals for Busy Witches
The Marshmallow Massacre: Halloween Treats with a Sinister Twist
Blood and Blackberry Thorns
Magickal Mornings: Rituals for a Blessed Christmas Day
Embers of the All-Hallows Fire
The Pumpkin Market Collapse
The Hour You Gained: Transforming Time Into Power
The Chamber Must Be Sealed: Mastering the Power of Controlled Access
The Cursed Manuscript of Petosiris
The Festive Hearth: Creating Holiday Traditions
Darkness Rising: Thriving as Nights Grow Longer
Harvesting Time: Turning the Year's End Into Your New Beginning

Petosiris and the 13th Zodiac Key
Wagewound: When Paychecks Become Identity Prisons
Walls That Watch
The Silent Feast: Rituals of Power in the Longest Night
The Distortus Legacy : Becoming a Deformed King in a Perfect World
The Hollow Masks
The Gratitude Furnace: Forging Gold from Thanks
Feast of Inner Gold: Eating for Energy and Enlightenment
Haunted Commerce: The Season of Spending Spirits
Fear Bonds: How Panic Creates Profit
Black Friday E-Commerce Playbook: Sales Tactics to Skyrocket Your Holiday Revenue
Budgeting for Black Friday: A Holiday Savings Planner
Haunting the Harvest Moon
The Warrior's Water: Emergency Preparedness for People With DI
The First Sip of the Year: A New Year's Survival Guide for Diabetes Insipidus
Doctor Who: The Thirteenth Node
The Unseen Struggle: Mental Health, Anxiety, and Chronic Thirst
The Hearth's Hidden Ledger: Counting Energies as Currency
The Gift Alchemist: Turning Any Offering Into Gold
The Papyrus of the Bound Spirit
The Magick of Leftovers: Transmutation in the Fridge
Frost and Fortune: Christmas Wealthcraft for the Modern Magus
Last-Minute Gifts: Creative Ideas on a Budget
10 Secrets to Surviving Holiday Crowds
The Witch's Dow Jones
The Witches' Graveyard Shift
Pumpkin Sigils: Carving Rites for Midnight Power

The Secret Shopper's Black Friday Guide: How to Get Early Access and VIP Deals

Fever in the Foundation

The Neuralyzer Reset: Reprogram Your Morning Routine

Lightning Lessons of the White Painted Woman

The Enchanted Snowflake

The Magic Sip: Surviving Disney Parks with Diabetes Insipidus

The One Who Draws Through You

Santa's Secrets: A Magical Holiday Planner

Silent Bells, Loud Miracles: Self-Help for the Season of Stillness

The Sugar Spell Codex: Confectionary Magick of Christmas

Autumn Hexcraft: Fallen Leaves, Fallen Barriers

Sleep Like a Fortress: Build a Life Where Insomnia Can't Survive

Nowhere Was Ever Home

Christmas Under the Stars: A Celestial Holiday Guide

Rentproof: How to Never Be Evicted Again

Workless: Escape the 9-5 Without Being Broke

The Gilded Gift: A Wealth Altar for Christmas Morning

The Black Friday Grimoire

The Hollowing: Ceremonies of Spiritual Collapse

Doctor Who: The Nameless Signal

Where the Eagle Hides His Courage

The Dwarf Tyrant's Ascent: Claiming Power in a World of Giants

The Currency of the Dead: Trading with Spectral Bankers

The Icebound Witch: Survival and Magick in the Cold

The Emergency Money Mind: Constant Crisis, Zero Calm

Thirst & Roses: A Valentine's Survival Guide for Diabetes Insipidus

Springing Into Clarity: Mastering the Energy Shift of Daylight Saving

Speed of the Nanotyrant: Agile Strategies for Life's Hunt

The 90-Day Reset: A Science-Backed Guide to Reinvent Yourself Before the New Year

The Coil of Thorns

Timegates Unleashed

Dopamine Fasting 2.0: Rewiring Your Brain in a World of Overstimulation

The Nanotyrannus Mutation: Embracing Your Differentiated Form

Unwritten January: How to Use the Blank Page of the Year to Re-Author Your Life

Feast of the Forgotten Spirits: Ancestor Magick for the Holidays

The Burnout Codex: A System for Thriving Beyond Stress

I Don't Deserve to Have Money

When the King Doesn't See You: The Shadow Predator's Guide

The Reset Ritual :A Guide to Shedding Last Year's Weight—Emotional and Physical—by Spring Cleaning Your Soul

Calendar Alchemy: Learn to Bend Time and Productivity around Your Natural Rhythms

The Mirror Contract: A One-Sentence Agreement with Yourself that Unlocks Real Change

The Nile Formula: Sacred Flow for Millionaire Minds

Forward Momentum: Productivity Rituals for the Lost Hour

Harvest Gold: Wealth Magick of Pumpkin Spice Commerce

The Magick of Christmas Lights: Illuminating Holiday Rituals

Cranberry Crown: Royal Self-Worth through Ritual Meals

Petosiris and the Worms of the Feathered Throne

The Evergreen Equation: Self-Help for Sustained Growth

The Rain Will Wash Us Away: Emo Weather Magick

Snowlight Shadows: Magick Under Frozen Stars

Doctor Who: Merger of Empires

The Light Within the Feast: Magickal Wealth of Yuletide Flame

Momentum Machines: Small Habits Designed to Snowball into Unstoppable Forward Motion

Calm Spells: Magickal Solutions for Anxiety Relief

Santa's Final List: The Naughty Never Leave

The Mystic's Guide to Banishing Worry

The Silence Dividend: Turning Quiet Mornings into Compounding Growth All Year

Charmed Stillness: Rituals to Ease the Mind

Blood Spiral Ascension

The Vanishing Heart Invocation

Crystal Calm: Harnessing Stones for Anxiety

The Nano Tyrant Code: Strength in the Small Predator

The Energy Ledger: Accounting Methods for Vitality, Not Just Money

Snowglobe Mindset: Shake Up Your Thoughts, Settle Into Peace

The Weight of the Feather: Anubis's Codes for Soul Balance

Pocket Peppermint Power: Tiny Rituals for Big Holiday Energy

Shadowkeeper of the Golden Jackal: Anubis's Path to Energetic Protection

The Witch's Breath: Anxiety Relief Through Magickal Breathing

The Tiny Ember: Pocket Motivation for Cold Days

Stocking Sorcery: Mini Spells for Holiday Luck and Prosperity

Warm Hands, Steady Heart: Micro Grounding for Winter Anxiety

The Jackal's Lantern: Guide-Lights for Walking the Dark Path

Anubis's Silent Steps: Rituals for Stealth, Peace & Emotional Quiet

The Bonewake Protocol

Extinction-Proof: How to Outlive Trends, Trauma, and Time

The Fourth Doctor: The Eccentric Wanderer

The Second Doctor: Chaos and Charm in the TARDIS (Patrick Troughton, 1966–1969)

The Third Doctor: Earthbound Defender of Time (Jon Pertwee, 1970–1974)

The First Doctor: Genesis of the Time Lord (William Hartnell, 1963–1966)

The Fourth Doctor: The Eccentric Wanderer *(Tom Baker, 1974–1981)*

The Fifth Doctor: Elegance and Empathy (Peter Davison, 1982–1984)

The Sixth Doctor: A Kaleidoscope of Conflict (Colin Baker, 1984–1986)

The Seventh Doctor: The Strategist of Shadows (Sylvester McCoy, 1987–1989)

The Eighth Doctor: A Time Lord's Renaissance (Paul McGann, 1996)

The War Doctor: A Time Lord's Burden (John Hurt, 2013)

The Ninth Doctor: The Healer of Worlds
(Christopher Eccleston, 2005)

The Tenth Doctor: The Lonely Hero (David Tennant, 2005–2010)

The Eleventh Doctor: The Madman in a Box (Matt Smith, 2010–2013)

The Twelfth Doctor: The Rebel with a Cause (Peter Capaldi, 2013–2017)

The Thirteenth Doctor: Breaking the Mold
(Jodie Whittaker, 2017–2022)

The Fourteenth Doctor: A New Beginning (David Tennant, 2022–2023)

The Fifteenth Doctor: Rewriting the Stars

(Ncuti Gatwa, 2023–2025)

Santa's Shortcut to Success: Micro Habits for a Better New Year

The Midnight Cocoa Manifesto: Comfort Rituals for Hard Nights

Why I Can't Save: Trauma Blocks to Financial Planning

Dino Brain, Mega Goals: Rewire Yourself for Savage Success.

Jurassic Profit: Unearth Your Inner Millionaire Fossil

Scales & Softness: Dating with Dino Heart

Carnotaurus Dreams.

Red Willow Thinking.

Reindeer Resilience: How to Keep Going When You're Exhausted

Candlewick Courage: Lighting Strength in Dark Seasons.

Elf-Mode Focus: Fast Attention Fixes for Busy Seasons

Futureproof Feelings: Emotional Skill-Building for Resilience No Matter What the New Year Brings

The 90-Day Rewire: Transform Your Neural Pathways Before Spring Blooms

Jolly Rich: Christmas Micro-Money Magick for Fast Prosperity.

Gingerbread Gratitude: Mini Practices for a Happier Holiday

Trauma-Spending: When Money Becomes a Drug

Get Some Tarot cards: https://www.makeplayingcards.com/sell/apophis-occult-shop

Get some shirts: https://www.bonfire.com/store/apophis-shirt-emporium/

Instagrams:
@apophis_enterprises,
@apophisbookemporium,
@apophisscardshop
Twitter: @apophisenterpr1
Tiktok:@apophisenterprise
Youtube: @sg1fan23477
Hive: @sg1fan23477
CheeLee: @SG1fan23477

Podcast: Apophis Chat Zone: https://open.spotify.com/show/5zXbrCLEV2xzCp8ybrfHsk?si=fb4d4fdbdce44dec

Newsletter: https://apophiss-newsletter-27c897.beehiiv.com/

If you want to support me or see posts of other projects that I have come over to: **buymeacoffee.com/mpetchinskg**

I post there daily several times a day

Get your Dinowicca or Christmas themed digital products, especially Santa Raptor songs and other musics. Here: **https://sg1fan23477.gumroad.com**

Apophis Yuletide Digital has not only digital Christmas items, but it will have all things with Dinowicca as well as other Digital products.

www.ingramcontent.com/pod-product-compliance
Lightning Source LLC
LaVergne TN
LVHW022013200926
848481LV00007B/2376